Hope
for the
Days Ahead

Jean Bufton

ISBN 978-1-64458-802-4 (paperback)
ISBN 978-1-64458-803-1 (digital)

Copyright © 2019 by Jean Bufton

All rights reserved. No part of this publication may be reproduced, distributed, or transmitted in any form or by any means, including photocopying, recording, or other electronic or mechanical methods without the prior written permission of the publisher. For permission requests, solicit the publisher via the address below.

Christian Faith Publishing, Inc.
832 Park Avenue
Meadville, PA 16335
www.christianfaithpublishing.com

Printed in the United States of America

Mary Bonaventura

This book would not have been written if it wasn't for my Aunt Mary. She was a Godly woman, devoted wife, mother, grand and great grandmother who loved her family. There was a radiance about her that I was drawn to. Her smile and words reflected the peace and joy she had in her heart. She had a deep abiding faith in a powerful God and loving Savior. It was because of her that I became a child of God. She led me to Jesus. Here is my expression of thanks to her.

> How can I say thanks for what you did for me me?
> You told me about Jesus and Calvary.
> The Son of God, one I never knew,
> In your sweet way, told me what to do.
> You said, "Receive Him into your heart this day.
> And that is where He will always stay."
> You shared from His word what I now know,
> John 3:16, Oh how He loved me so.

I will never forget that glorious day,
When I found Jesus was the only way.
I came to the Father through Jesus, His son!
It's the only way it can be done.
Not through riches, works, or deeds.
It was his grace that set me free.
It was then I became a child of God!
And with great pleasure He did nod,
"My child, you have come to me today,
Now go tell others, this is the way."
So it's with great joy I share this story,
Giving God all of the glory.

Golie Robinson

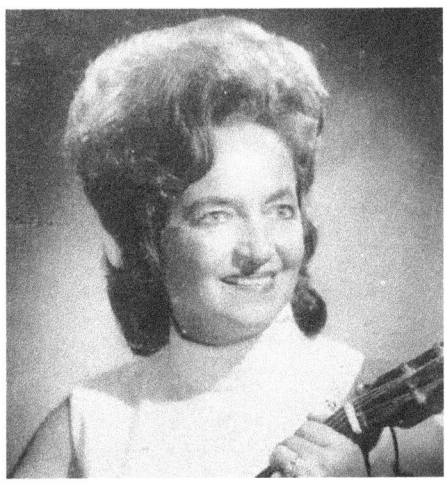

God sends many angel's into our lives at just the right time. This is to help us grow in our walk with the Lord. I am so thankful that He knew what I needed and sent me Golie Robinson, a dear Christian singer, speaker, and Bible teacher. If it were not for her, I would not be where I am today in my Christian walk. She became my "Spiritual Mother." I had so much to learn. She taught me how to live the victorious Christian Life – with the power of the Holy Spirit, the power of joy and praise, the power of positive prayer, and the power of witnessing. The most important was the power of finding joy in trusting God in every circumstance, which is the heartbeat of this book. Then and only then can you live Joyfully in Jesus!

Each of these dear ladies have been God's gift to me. They have been put in my life at just the right time. Oh how I Praise the Lord for each one of them. Their stories are shared in detail throughout these pages. I am sure you will be blessed by their positive insights, power in prayer, and God's priceless promises.

Florence Littauer

Florence is an excellent speaker, dynamic communicator, seminar leader, Bible teacher and author of over thirty best selling books. She and her daughter Marita developed Class Speakers, Inc. which is the training and development of Christian leaders and speakers. I had the privilege of attending the first Class Seminar in 1984 at their home in Redlands, California. It was through their teaching, sharing, mentoring, and personal guidance that enhanced my desire to speak and then to write this book. I will be forever grateful to Florence, Marita, and their staff for the vision and dedication in helping me, and many other women and men to develop their skills in speaking and writing.

We met Florence and her husband Fred in 1982. They were the speakers at a Marriage Seminar that we were attending in Indiana. We had an instant rapport and connection, a "God thing" for sure. Bill and I were just starting our Ministry with couples and giving marriage seminars. They took us under their wings and became our mentors and good friends through the years.

Contents

Dedication iii
Acknowledgments 11
Testimonials 13
Chapter Outline 17
Introduction 25

Acknowledgments

I am overwhelmed and in awe as I hold this book in my hand, and realize what God has done. When I think of what our lives were like, and what they could have been, I give God all the glory. We are walking, living miracles of His unconditional love—Amazing Grace—forgiveness and faithfulness. It is with great joy and praise that I share my story in this book with you. I am thanking the Lord for all that He has done and will continue to do, knowing that "with God all things are possible!"

After the Lord, I want to thank my husband, Bill, for all that he has done. This could not have been completed if it wasn't for his constant support, affirmation, and encouragement as I was writing this book. It was completed through endless hours of critiquing and changes that needed to be made. He handled all of the computer entries, corrections, along with the proofing and editing. Bill would patiently read and reread the pages over and over to me, making sure that they were correct. He also co-authored the chapters on "Parenting" and "Finances," and he is a big part of all that has been accomplished. We have been in full-time ministry since we founded Heartline Ministries in 1994. During that period we have given retreats and seminars for married couples and families along with countless hours of counseling. What a blessing it has been to serve the Lord together.

To include everyone who has had a part in making this possible would be impossible. It would be another chapter.

ACKNOWLEDGMENTS

However, I do want to acknowledge a few more, our parents and family. My parents, Carlo and Irma DeRango, and two sisters, Jeri, Debbie, and family. Bill's parents, John and Ollie Bufton, sister Gerry, Marvin, and family. Of course our children, grandchildren, and great grandchildren have made all of this worthwhile. They are our joy and blessings in life and we thank the Lord for each of them.

We are grateful for all of our friends, prayer warriors, prayer partners, and church families. There are too many to name, but you know who you are. You have been the main heartbeat and foundation of this book being completed. No words could ever be sufficient to share our heartfelt thanks for you. We praise the Lord for your faithful love, prayers, concern, and care for us. I have said it before and I will say it again, we would not be where we are today if it weren't for all of you. May God richly bless you for blessing us.

To Kecia and Kathy who both typed and retyped the first and second draft of the manuscripts. I thank you with a grateful heart for the endless hours of patiently "putting it on paper" so it would become a reality. This was no easy task as I handed it to you on yellow legal pads, written in red with no periods, commas, punctuations, or paragraphs. Bless you both for your labor of love!

Through a series of circumstances that only God could have arranged, this book is being published. He led us to *Christian Faith Publishers* in Meadville, PA. We were pleased with their professionalism, policies and staff. From the first contact with Kathleen to Jordyn our publication specialist. We were blessed by the entire staff at *CFP*. We would like to convey our thanks for all you have done to complete this book.

Testimonials

"I have known Bill and Jean Bufton for decades. During that time, I've repeatedly prompted them to write their story as I knew it would be an encouragement to many – I saw in them what they could not see in themselves. I am grateful to now know that the seed I planted in them long ago has finally borne fruit. People today still need hope – perhaps even more so than when my husband and I first crossed paths with the Buftons. The pages of "Hope for the Days ahead" are filled with understanding, compassion, and a touch of humor that offers encouragement no matter what difficulties you may be facing. I'm honored that my work has played such an important role in the Buftons story – which is so similar to that of my husband and me. Applying the principles offered within these pages will confirm that you are not alone and that there is "Hope for the Days ahead."

Florence Littauer – Author of dozens of books including
After Every Wedding Comes a Marriage
and *Personality Plus* - Texas

TESTIMONIALS

"Jean has been my friend for over 30 years and I know you will not find anyone more sincere and enthusiastic in desire to serve up relational hope. If your heart hurts, Jean cares. You"ll sense it on every page.

> Patsy Clairmont – Speaker– Author "You Are More Than You Know."- Tennessee

"Jean is known and loved for her unwavering witness for Christ and her gentle wise counsel. Her book, *"Hope For The Days Ahead"* leaves one feeling as though you are sharing a cup of coffee with a Titus 2 woman of faith. Jean shares how she trusted God through the challenges of each chapter of her life and how God faithfully went before her and with her."

> Donna R. Tyson – Inspirational speaker – Missionary – author – *"The Red Bow"* - South Carolina

"What a privilege it has been through the years to have been instrumental in the lives of Bill and Jean Bufton. They have a heart for those who are hurting along with a powerful impact on everyone they meet. They share from their personal testimonies, along with God's word in a dynamic and powerful way. Throughout this book, you can see how God has used them in ministry. Both of them have the charisma and compassion that allows them to relate to anyone who needs "Hope for the Days ahead."

> Rev. Jim Counihan – Evangelist – President - Jim Counihan Ministry - Arizona

"Some of the greatest burdens that people carry in our day are the burdens of hurt and pain from the past. Bill and Jean Bufton have made it a personal mission in their lives to move people into a closer relationship with God and others by living the concept of receiving God's love, acceptance, and salvation into their lives. Bill and Jean live out what they have written. They are examples for other believers and witnesses to those who have not yet met Christ in a personal way. What a blessing they were to the church of which I was Pastor and now friends of my wife Dee and me for more than thirty years."

> Dr. Robert Ricker – Pastor - President – Baptist General Conference - California

Chapter 1:   Marriage: Mission Impossible 27

Our experience was similar to so many marriages today. I can relate to the hurt and broken hearts when all of the love and respect is gone and needs are not being met. In fact, in most cases, they are just existing together. Our relationship was like this and was compounded with extreme differences in our religious beliefs and backgrounds. My husband and I were opposite in every way. After seven years of trying to make it on our own, we gave up. We both needed help! Does this sound like a hopeless situation? It was. That's why this chapter is so significant in setting the foundation for the rest of the book. In it, you will see how we had a glimmer of hope, and this seemingly impossible situation became possible with God.

Chapter 2:   Marriage in Crisis: Handle with Care 40

By the seventh year of our marriage, we were in major crisis. Most marriages reach that point for various reasons such as personal differences that cause conflicts, lack of communication or no communication, no commitment, infidelity, loss of a job, or the death of a child. These circumstances, complicated by everyday difficulties, cause crisis situations. In some cases, severe trials can draw a family closer; but in most cases, it tears them apart. How do we handle these with care? There is only one way—with Christ in our lives. This chapter will reveal the transforming truths that changed our lives, confirming that a marriage can be restored, love can be renewed, and a relationship can be revitalized.

CHAPTER OUTLINE

Chapter 3:   S---------: Ugh! That Dreaded Word!............54

There was a day when that word was not even in my vocabulary. I went into our marriage determined that I was not going to submit to my husband. So many women feel this way today because they do not have a clear understanding of the word "submission." In this chapter, I very clearly define what submission is and what submission is not. It is definitely not being a doormat, becoming downtrodden, or being subject to physical abuse. When I learned this and the true definition from the Word of God, it set me free to be in loving submission to my husband as unto the Lord. What a difference in our actions and attitude toward our husbands when we know this.

Chapter 4:   Hang On! We're Headed for Happiness!......69

I remember the time when we were settled and content in our "Christian comfort zone." We were in the perfect house in the perfect neighborhood, had the perfect job, and our kids were in the perfect school. We were also in the perfect social situation, had wonderful friends, and were happy and busy ministering in our church. Everything was going along so well, and then we got a nudge from the Lord to move. Could we really leave all of this and follow him? My husband said yes, and I said, "Oh maybe." This is a hilarious happening on how I had to let go of my grip and let God take me on a trip. Hang on, we're headed for happiness; this will be a joyful journey.

**Chapter 5: A Great Discovery: We Can Be
Different and Not Be Wrong 86**

The information in this chapter absolutely changed our lives! For years, Bill and I fought for position and control—compromise was not an option. We never agreed, and each of us thought the other was wrong. We were definitely two opposite people who were attracted to each other, and right after the wedding, started to attack one another. This went on in a milder form even after we became Christians. What a revelation to discover the four basic temperaments and to realize that we can be different and not wrong. These truths revolutionized our relationship with each other as well as with our children, family, and friends. I guarantee that it will be life changing for anyone who reads about the temperaments and applies them to their life in the appropriate way.

Chapter 6: Help! I'm a Parent! 100

I know of no more important calling that comes with a greater privilege and overwhelming responsibility than that of being a parent. Some parents do not have a clue about what to do or how to raise their children. Bill and I were young parents, and we were not Christians when we were raising our three children, so we know how difficult this can be. Are you having family feuds or family fun? This chapter will give hope to parents, godly principles, and some helpful guidelines. Yes, God does have a plan. The ideal is to start when they are young, but we feel that it is never too late. You can turn your frustration into firmness and family fun!

CHAPTER OUTLINE

Chapter 7:   From Fiscal Failure to Financial Freedom: That Makes Good Cents 111

We have been in both "feast or famine" situations. We have been rolling in dough and scraping the bottom of the barrel. We've had the top dollar and the last dollar, being a day late and a dollar short with payments. Yes, we understand and can relate to the average family especially in this uncertain economical situation we are in. This chapter includes resources and a revised plan for restoration and recovery in the area of finances. Yes, God will meet our needs, but He wants us to be "cents-able," resourceful, and fiscally responsible with His money. This does make "good cents!"

Chapter 8:   Let's Replace Fear for Faith 122

Fear is not funny. It is frightening and comes in all forms relating to our family, future, failures, finances, etc. In this chapter, I will address these areas of fear with a little different approach. I show how these fearful thoughts are lies and deceptions from the enemy in an attempt to paralyze us and lose sight of our faith in God. He states 365 times throughout the Bible, one for every day, "Fear not, I am with you!" When fear causes paralysis, it's faith that gives us power. I feel by exchanging these negative thoughts with positive promises, we can begin to replace fear with faith. No, it's not easy, but it can be done. This chapter gives the formula for this freedom.

**Chapter 9:   Lord, I Need a Friend Like You with
                Arms to Hug Me 131**

One of the greatest needs in the Christian life is a true friend. If you have one, you are fortunate. If you have more, you are extremely blessed. I feel they are definitely a special gift from God, and I feel privileged to have many. In this chapter, not only would I like to pay tribute to these precious friends, but to give some creative ways to be a special friend, and establish friendships, be instrumental in bringing people together as friends, and ways to form friendship groups. There are many lonely women everywhere, even in your church, who need a friend like Jesus with arms to hug them. You can be their example of Jesus who is a friend that sticks closer than a brother.

Chapter 10:   California, Here We Come! 150

The mountain looks pretty high from the valley we were in. We left for California in 1985, hurting but with high hopes, little money, and no job. We did have a lot of trust. Only the Lord could have been directing us as we took this step of faith. This chapter explains what it's like to literally be in the "valley" for months, those times when you don't even get a glimpse of the mountaintop. But Lord, we sure were tired of looking at those weeds! Many people are in those same valleys these days and need to know that there is *Hope for the Days Ahead* even in those devastating valley circumstances.

CHAPTER OUTLINE

Chapter 11: Lord, Can You Change the Dial on This Time of Trial? 167

I believe trusting is the hardest thing to do in the Christian life—that complete surrender and relinquishing of our will and control. Trusting our unknown future to someone we can't even see, but have the belief that He is an all-knowing, loving God, and always knows what is best for us.

Through many trials and life experiences, I will show you how trusting is the key to complete victory. It begins with faith, but trust is the action word because you have to do it. You make the choice. Yes, many times, we would like to change the dial when we see a trial come. This chapter will reveal how to take our trials and turn the dial to trust. Not high, low, cool, medium, or hot. No, it's that steady, unmovable, consistent temperature of trust.

Chapter 12: Let's Synchronize Our Watches, Lord 181

I felt God's timing wasn't ticking with my clock. God's timing is never the same as ours. Yes, we can make our plans, but the final outcome is always in His hands.

This chapter is a perfect example of that, and through our "Atlanta adventure" experience, I know it will give hope to those who just don't understand why certain things are happening at this time in their lives. It will bring a whole new dimension of trusting God's plan and will for your life. You will also learn to say yes even though you don't know what the outcome will be especially if you are going into full-time ministry.

**Chapter 13: When in the Pits of Pain, Peace
             Comes Only through Prayer......................198**

I have experienced all types of emotional pain in my life and can relate to those who are in similar situations. Yes, and with great empathy, I can minister to them and give them *Hope for the Days Ahead*. I have also prayed at the bedside of those who were suffering with physical pain, but I never knew exactly how they felt. I had a crash course in September of 1992 and found out about that type of pain. I must say, pain took on a whole new perspective for me. Yes, while I was in the pits of it, I learned the purpose for it and experienced God's provisions in it. This chapter will convey how even when we are paralyzed in pain, through prayer, we can feel His power, peace, and His presence in us. Then we can accept His plan for us.

**Chapter 14: Please Send Help, Lord. I'm Really
             Hurting 211**

I have never seen such hopelessness and so many hurting people as in these last days. People everywhere need help. I believe we have the answer and can help them and give them hope. In my closing chapter, I conclude with confidence where that help comes from, hope to receive it, hang on to it, apply it to your life, and share it with others. God does turn hurting, broken hearts into "healed helpers." I personally have experienced the victory and freedom this hope brings. Yes, even in the most difficult circumstances, we can have *Hope for the Days Ahead!*

Meet Our Family...215

Introduction

*H*ope for the Days Ahead will not be based on the world situation or our circumstances, finances, future, or family, because these will disappoint us. It will not be based on a *"feeling"* of what we want or what will happen as *Webster's Dictionary* describes it. But, rather, the *fact* that hope is a constant expectation of a promised blessing, not present or seen, but real and distinct, as *Wycliffe* describes it. Our hope can only be found in the Lord and His promises for us in His Word. Romans 5:5 says, "This hope does not disappoint us." Hope plays a vital part in the lives of believers. We need this hope in the day-to-day pain and pressure of life in times of doubts, fears, failures, lack of faith, and especially when anticipating your future. Psalm 39:7 says, "Lord, our only hope is in you."

Take this journey with me and you will see how you can have:

* Healing for your hurts
* Peace in your pain
* Trust in your trials
* Sufficiency in your suffering
* Faith in your fears
* Miracles in your marriage
* Contentment with your children
* Confidence in your crisis
* Joy in your journey

God wants to fill you with His peace and joy. As it says in Romans 15:13, "Now the God of hope fill you with all joy and peace in believing, that you may abound in hope through the power of the Holy Spirit."

This book is written with that hope and Joy-fully in Jesus,

Jean Bufton
Contact – e-mail – jbbufton@yahoo.com

Chapter 1

Marriage: Mission Impossible

Florence Littauer has written an excellent book titled *After Every Wedding Comes a Marriage*. It is a true statement and a reality in the lives of most couples. When all the excitement of planning it and the wedding day is over, you are faced with a marriage and wonder, "What do we do now?"

This chapter will definitely give you *Hope for the Days Ahead* in your marriage. If you are thinking about marriage or if you just became engaged, please read on! If you are in your first to seventh year of marriage, please don't put this book down. This may save your life and your marriage. If you have passed or barely survived that very crucial seventh year—the seven-year itch as it is called—and are just existing and going through the motions of marriage, read on for dear life. There is hope and new life to be found! If you are in the angry, independent, self-sufficient stages of not caring and have the "you go your way and I'll go mine" attitude, you won't want to miss this story. If you are thinking, "Yes, my marriage is in the 'mission impossible' stage," please continue on. Maybe you have made a decision to walk out and are considering divorce, please stay one more day and read this chapter. I really believe you will be surprised to hear our outcome as we have walked through every one of these stages in our marriage.

As I take you through the years of our lives, you will see how God's love *can* change two people's lives, how your relationship can be renewed, and your marriage can be restored and revitalized. You will see how our mission impossible became possible with God.

Let me take you back to the good old days—the fifties—to a small community in the Midwest where Bill and I were born and raised. The Tri-City area consists of LaSalle, Peru, and Oglesby in Illinois located about one hundred miles southwest of Chicago. In 1957, we were high school sweethearts and were busy going to football and basketball games, cheerleading, going on hayrides, picnics, and to the prom. It was the era of bobby socks and saddle shoes, crew cuts and ponytails, poodle skirts and hip-huger jeans. Elvis Presley was popular then, and we were having fun dancing the "Jitterbug" and the "Twist." On the whole, we had a great time and had some fond memories.

Things seemed so simple then; nothing like what our teenagers are facing today. Times have changed drastically, especially regarding marriage and children. The norm in the fifties was to go steady, get engaged, get married right after graduation, have children, and live happily ever after. It was just the thing to do back then, and that was what Bill and I did.

We decided to get married at the young ages of nineteen and twenty-one for what we thought were two very important reasons. Number one was that we were *so* in love. Maybe some of you can relate. Remember when you were so in love that nothing else mattered? It didn't matter that you came from two different backgrounds and religious upbringings or that you were opposite in every way. The differences were what we were attracted to. It didn't matter if you had different goals and dreams in life, or that you were raised completely differently.

No, this didn't matter because you two were so in love and that love was going to overcome any problem.

The second reason we decided to get married was that everyone else was. It was part of the typical fifties lifestyle. On these two firm foundations we started on this lifelong trip and what a trip it was. From Valentine's Day to graduation during our senior year, one by one, couples would announce their engagements. Then the wedding plans began, and excitement filled the air. Dates were set for summer weddings, and shopping for dresses began. Invitations ordered, reception halls reserved, and caterers contacted. As friends, we all took part in each other's weddings, and it was fun giving showers and sharing the anticipation of the big day. All of our preparations focused on the wedding, and we honestly didn't think of much past that except for the honeymoon, of course. At that time, there were no pre-marital seminars or any idea of roles and responsibilities. We didn't think about meeting each other's needs or planning for a family. There were no basic instructions, and no one gave us advice on finances or budgets. We just planned the wedding, got married, and found out very quickly that yes, *After Every Wedding Comes a Marriage.*

I heard the saying recently that marriage is like a wake-up call; after the "ring," you wake up. Instantly, right after the "ring," you wake up next to a stranger thinking, *Who is this person I married?* When you are dating, you are always on your best behavior doing and saying things you know will please each other in your concern to make a good impression. You sacrifice your interests, going places you know will make your partner happy, attending ball games, sports events, musicals, plays, etc. You know the old game we play to make someone become interested in us, or performance-based acceptance as we know it today.

Bill and I discovered on our honeymoon that we were the exact opposite. Yes, our honeymoon was the beginning of our discovery that we did not have anything in common. We were opposites, and we could not agree on anything!

It is so funny when you *seriously* think of the little things that add up and cause such conflicts. The best example is that trivial tube of toothpaste. Grounds for divorce for sure! Everywhere we go, wherever we speak, we get the biggest response from the toothpaste trauma. In my case, I'm the "roller," and Bill is the "squeezer!" And yes, the next morning on our honeymoon, there was that brand new tube of toothpaste squeezed from the center left *open* on the sink with the cap nowhere to be found. Yuck! *Oh no!* I thought. *I'll change that real quick, and this will definitely stop*!

The room was freezing, just the way Bill liked it. He was comfortable if it was shivering cold in the bedroom, and I liked it warm. Funny, after age fifty, things change. Now I'm warm all of the time, and Bill is cold. Ha! Anyway, I glanced around the room, and I saw a sight. I could not believe my eyes—clothes, shoes, socks, Bill's tie, jacket, everything was strewn and draped all over the room. This "neat as a pin" man I dated and thought I had married was a clothes "flipper," leaving them wherever they happened to fall. Yes, in every family, there is a flipper or a folder, a tosser or a hanger, a squeezer or a roller, a freezer or a sweater. Are you relating at all? I think that every couple we talk to or counsel has this problem. I really thought that these irritations were just going to be temporary, but they did continue.

Our honeymoon was a relaxed, casual time in which I was having a real problem adjusting to because I am the type of person who likes to have every minute well planned with fun activities (I like organized fun). And Bill is the type of person who flies by the seat of his pants—no schedule, no map, no pre-registrations, no pre-arranged reservations. He just "wings" it. Are you getting the picture of a potential problem here? Very definitely! Several problems in fact. I was making my list of *all* the changes we were going to make when we got home (or maybe that *I* was going to have *Bill* make), and I could not wait! In spite of all of our different ideas, we did manage to have a fun honeymoon. Not planned or organized, but fun.

Our first post-honeymoon horror was the clothes conflict; and I saw immediately that this was not just a honeymoon flight but a faithful habit, which, I might add, has continued for fifty-some years and is getting better this year. I always say I have an answer to many things, but I do not have an answer on how to get your husband to pick up his clothes. One woman came up to me after a seminar I had conducted and said, "Be happy he is there to pick up after." I did have a quiver of guilt. Somehow, even as shocking as that sounded, I could not relate at the moment. But I did tell her that I would pass that information on and have every time I've spoken.

Then, of course, we had the classic toothpaste test. We have finally, after many years of marriage, taken care of this problem with the no-drip tubes of toothpaste. Thank you, toothpaste industry, for saving so many marriages! Oh, and of course, one other little issue that needs to be discussed and agreed on before marriage, and after the toothpaste, is the other big *T*—the toilet paper. Without going into too much detail, I am just going to say that *over* is right (check the printed pattern!). Now I know to some it really does not make any difference, but to *many*, it does! I happen to be one of the many and, of course, Bill has given in to that. Only occasionally, like right before we are scheduled to speak and he knows I am going to use this illustration, he will deliberately turn it under so I will notice and have a fit about it. Does it really make a difference? Well, it is not a matter of life or death, but I know for a fact that it does cause problems. These differences piled up on a ton of others make for one unhappy homemaker.

Our differences were not uncommon, but they did go on and on. He liked big cars and I liked small ones. He liked steak and I liked fish. He liked Coke and I chose Sprite. He liked sports and I didn't. He liked to relax and I liked to work. I would embellish a story to make it colorful and interesting, and he wanted "just the facts."

Our biggest differences were our family backgrounds and religious beliefs. I came from an Italian-Catholic home. Bill came from a conservative, English-Baptist home. Not only were the religious beliefs so opposite, but the way we were raised in all aspects—the way we celebrated birthdays and holidays, the preparation of meals, the way we entertained, and more.

These are the typical shocks you face immediately after the wedding. Combine all of these with different temperaments and, of course, financial problems. The way we handled our money was extremely different. As you can see, as in most marriages, we had different opinions in every area of our lives.

Remember that love you had way back in the beginning, the love that was going to overcome everything? Well, our love did not cover our rent payments, car payments, electric bills, or insurance. We had three children under four years old, so I had to quit my job and Bill had to get a part-time job just to make ends meet. I remember sometimes having twenty-five cents left over from payday to payday. Tough times, yes. With Bill working two jobs, he would come home from one, eat quickly, and then go to the other, getting home late and very tired. We were not meeting each other's needs. Actually, to be honest, we did not even know how to meet each other's needs, or even what that meant.

As we look back, Bill thought he was meeting my needs because he was working hard and *providing* the material things

I needed. In our parent's era, providing material things was enough. This was a big thing with most men. It was important for Bill to have a nice home, car, clothes, etc. Whereas for me, those "things" did not matter. I needed emotional security and understanding, as most women do. He needed affirmation and appreciation for *all* he was doing to give us what he thought we needed. What a terrible state we were in.

Times are even more difficult today economically. The average family is struggling to survive, and many people do not even have an income they can depend on. I do understand the desperation you must feel not only financially, but also as a wife and mother; I was in your shoes.

We had three children in the first four years of our marriage. I know what it is like to be home all day with small children and the demands that involves. Yes, you do get weary from being Supermom all day—working, cleaning, changing diapers, wiping noses, talking baby talk, chauffeuring kids to school, attending meetings, helping with homework, making lunches, and all the rest. Just a normal day in the "happy housewife" routine.

If you are a mom who works outside of your home, it is just as hard for you to cope, but in a different way. Getting up and getting everyone off to day care, working in the business world all day with all of those demands and stresses, and then coming home and wearing your "wife and mother" hat. This is not easy either. Picture all of this and then add the husband who has worked all day with demanding deadlines, frazzled from fighting the typical pressures of his rat-race job. Now bring these two people and two or three small children together at six o'clock, and what do you have? A family crying out, "Help! I need you!" and demanding undivided attention. Each one with individual needs and not much to give because they are maxed out themselves. This is the state we find in the counseling office of so many families today.

This was the case with Bill and me. I could not wait for him to come home so I could relate with and talk to an adult who would listen to me as I shared my concerns and crises of the day. Yes, I needed my knight in shining armor to sweep through the door and say, "Here I am! I love you! How can I help you? I'm here for you. I understand you." Well, that may be a little exaggerated; but a smile, maybe a look, some recognition and appreciation for *all* that I did *all* day. Maybe even a pat on the back or a hug would have been great, just something to let me know that he cared.

Well, as you can imagine, Bill would come home from working two jobs, and he was not ready to rescue me. He had already heard people talking and complaining all day. He was not thrilled that I had three thousand words to share with him. (Actually, as fast as I talk, he knew it would be six thousand!) No, he did not want to hear my chattering and complaining. He wanted to come home and zone himself out with the television and the sports page for about half an hour and then take a half-hour nap. He would then want to eat dinner, play with the kids (maybe), and after they were in bed, he wanted me to be Superwife—romantic, loving, caring, calm, and cheerful. Yes, he needed to be pampered and appreciated for working so hard all day to provide the things he felt were important.

You become so weary and worn out, you don't have anything to give anymore. You become two empty, frustrated, tired people going through the motions of marriage and being totally unfulfilled. You become self-sufficient and independent. You blame the other person, which is so typical and easy to do. We see these symptoms in 90 percent of marriages today.

What do you do at this point? I will tell you what I did. Because we thought finances were our biggest problem, I decided to fulfill a lifelong dream and become a licensed beautician. My sincere motive was to supplement our income. The idea of accomplishing something for myself sounded good.

Therefore, after being a hassled housewife for four years, I enrolled in cosmetology school. My plans were to have a beauty shop in our home and help with the expenses. I will say that Bill did watch the kids at night during the week. With the help of our parents and close friends, I was able to attend school part-time and finish in eighteen months.

I did make more money, but it seemed like the more we made, the more we spent. We were in a terrible mess. We *really* wanted to be happy, but we did not know how. Our life was like a big puzzle with the main piece missing. What were we missing?

We thought if we bought more "things," we would be happy. Bill thought that if he bought a new car, he would be happy (he did and he wasn't). He thought if he bought a new carpet for our home or clothes for me that I would be happy (he did and I wasn't). We both thought that if we bought the children more toys, they would be happy (we did and they weren't). We knew if we had a new home, moved to a new neighborhood, we would *all* be happy (we did and we weren't). In fact, it was worse because we went further into debt, causing more stress and pressure on our relationship. Like many other married couples, we found that material things alone do not bring you peace and happiness. We found that you cannot put a price tag on happiness. Now that does not mean that you cannot have nice things in life because we know that God does bless and allows us to, but only when our priorities are in order.

I do not know how we ever got through the "seven year itch" of married life. This seems to be the most dangerous year in a marriage. From the fifth to the seventh, we find it to be a crucial turning point—for better or for worse. The novelty has worn off, the commitment has faded, and the responsibilities are overwhelming. Children and financial pressures only add fuel to the fire. Needs are not being met, and most couples are just going through the motions of being married.

Our "itch" was so bad that there was no cure, and it became very irritating. We were not only ruining our lives, but those around us, especially our children. It is very hard for me to say that, but it is true. When you are having problems, it does *affect* your children. Your parents, family, and, of course, your friends all feel it too.

When I look back, I can hardly believe all that we went through—all of the hurt and heartache, all the tears and the wasted years, all of the selfishness and arguing. We were caught in a trap and did not know how to get out. We had lost all of our love and respect for one another. We did not even like each other. We were going our separate ways yet staying together mostly for the children. How many marriages are like that today, just existing and going through the motions? Most of them are Christians who stay together for religious reasons, living in an unhappy marriage. We call that type of co-existing a Christian Divorce.

Is there hope when seemingly, all hope is gone? Hope for reconciliation, renewing and revitalizing your relationship? We are here to say a hearty yes! Yes, there is hope for the hassled housewife, frustrated father, and frazzled family. We do have some suggestions for survival and some serious steps toward having a successful marriage and ultimately, a satisfying relationship.

Now I wish I could say there was an instant solution, and with one snap of the finger and one swish of a spiritual wand, you could see a spontaneous, spectacular change; but it is not that simple! The instant "quick fix" scenario does not work here. It takes time. Remember, it took time and years and tears to get us there, and it is going to take time to change and rearrange those old patterns. If you want change in your home, it has to start with you.

I know what you may be thinking: "Why *me*? Why does it *always* have to be me?" I don't know why, but in *most* cases, it is *usually* the wife who changes first. I know some women resent that and will not even consider it. But I know when I came to this point in my marriage, I wanted to make this work.

I looked at my options, and I did not have to look any farther than the faces of my children. There they were—three precious, innocent children. Were their lives worth a sacrifice on my part? My answer was, "Yes! Whatever it takes, I will do it!" At that moment, I made a choice that changed the rest of our lives.

My simple but life-changing advice to you is found in three words: choice, commitment, and counsel. Some of you do not have a clue as to what to do or where to start. Some of you will want to, and some will not. (But if you did not want to change or have hope, you would not be reading this. Go with that desire for change.) The *choice* is up to you. For those who do, here are some simple steps, one built on the other, making a firm family foundation:

1. *Choice*

    You definitely have to make a choice. This is not easy because usually, your heart says one thing, your head says another, and your feelings say still another. So you have to set all of these aside and simply choose to change, as I did, based on what is best for *all* of your family. You have to make a choice to *stay*, a choice to *change*, and a choice to let go of the *control* of your life. Like Jesus in the Garden of Gethsemane, you must make a *choice* to accept "not *my* will God, but Yours," a *choice* to actually turn over the care of your life and unknown future to an *all*-knowing God. This will not be easy, and it will not happen overnight. If you choose to stay and trust God, He *will* honor your choice and be with you through your journey.

2. *Commitment*

I believe commitment is the most important word in marriage. Most people think it is *love*, but I must disagree. This word is seldom spoken anymore. It seems to have been forgotten or deleted from the marriage vocabulary and the English language. There is very little commitment between husbands and wives, parents and children, or even between employer and employee, for that matter. The general attitude is do your own thing; and if it does not work out, leave, quit, or just give up! Because there is no solid commitment, couples leave their spouses because they say they do not "love" each other anymore, or they do not have any feelings any more. I remember being in that situation, knowing our feelings for each other were gone. That love we felt when we first got married was not holding us together. In fact, it did not last very long at all.

We just cannot make that decision based on our feelings. Feelings are not going to be the firm foundation for your marriage, but facts are. The fact is that you can *choose* to make a *commitment* to make your marriage work. Psalm 37:5 states, "Commit everything you do to the Lord." Only with His help will this work. Christ's love and power working in us and through us make the difference in our will and actions during this changing process.

3. *Counsel*

"Seek the advice and counsel of others" (Prov. 15:22). We all need someone to talk to. May I suggest you find a godly woman, counselor, or friend who you can meet with on a regular basis? This should be someone you can trust, relate to, and share openly with, seeking answers from the scriptures and affirming God's principles for the family.

The family was God's idea, and He does have a plan for us. There are *many, many* good biblical-based counselors. I would suggest you attend selected retreats and/or seminars in your area for women. You can call your local church, or Focus on the Family for support groups. They will direct you to the proper place as you pursue the pathway to learning the practical "how to's" to help in your particular situation. This is what we did, and Bill and I are living examples of how two people who can be totally opposite, come from different backgrounds and religions, having nothing in common, and actually just existing in a state of matrimony, can make it!

In chapter 2, I will share with you how I made the *choice* to stay in my marriage, made the *commitment* to make it work, and sought the *counsel* of a godly woman. This marriage in crisis and mission impossible became possible with God. "With God all things are possible" (Matt. 19:26).

Chapter 2

Marriage in Crisis: Handle with Care

Bill and I went from a seven-year itch to a major crisis. When things were tough, we went from buying things to taking trips, trying to find happiness. We were trying to fix our failing marriage, but we did not know how. Serious decisions were being considered. We planned what we thought might be our last trip together. We thought if we could get away, we could think things through and see things more clearly. We decided to take a trip to California, land of sunshine, palm trees, and cool ocean breezes. We loved California. It was one of our favorite places to visit.

While we were there, we visited my Aunt Mary Bonaventura. Oh my, I wish you *all* could have met her. You would have loved her. She was special and very different from anyone I knew. There was a radiance about her that I was drawn to. When she spoke, her eyes lit up as her precious smile reflected the peace she had in her heart. I thought to myself, *Why is she so happy?* Actually, it was more than happiness. It was a presence of joy and peace from within. I quickly realized that her happiness did not depend on things, circumstances, or surroundings. It was different, like a deep contentment in her inner being—her soul.

She had a wonderful family—six children, and many grandchildren and great-grandchildren. Oh, how they loved her. When they were together, you could see the love they had for one another. This type of love did not depend on what she owned, but who she was: a woman of God, a devoted wife, a loving mother, and a prayerful great/grandmother. Here she was, very content in her lovely, modest home with simple surroundings and all of the basic necessities in life. But most of all, this unusual, deep, powerful love for her Lord and her family. I was drawn to that and wanted that happiness she had.

I kept thinking, *Bill and I have three beautiful, healthy, normal children and all of the material things the world told us we needed to be happy, but we still are not.* I asked my Aunt Mary what we were missing, and I will never forget her response. She said, "You are missing the love and life found in Jesus Christ." She shared these truths found in God's Word:

"For God loved the world so much that He gave His only Son so that anyone who believes in Him shall not perish but have eternal life" (John 3:16).

"Yes, all have sinned; all fall short of the Glory of God" (Rom. 3:23).

"For the wages of sin is death, but the free gift of God is eternal life through Jesus Christ our Lord" (Rom. 6:23).

"Because of His grace, you have been saved through trusting Christ. And even trusting is not of yourselves; it too is a gift from God. Salvation is not a reward for the good we have done, so none of us can take any credit for it"

Salvation is a gift from God—*free*—something we do not deserve, but because of His grace, which is unmerited favor, we can have it. But as any gift, we have to receive it (Eph. 2:8–9).

"But to as many as receive Him to them He gives the privilege to become His children" (John 1:12).

"And what is it that God has said? That He has given us eternal life, and that this life is in His Son. So whoever has God's Son has life; whoever does not have His Son, does not have life. I have written this to you who believe in the Son of God so that you may know you have eternal life" (1 John 5:11–13).

I could not believe it! All my life I believed in God. I had prayed and gone to church, but I had never heard these words before. God loved *me*, Christ died for *me*. "Not by works, but by faith alone are we saved and then we can *know* that we will have eternal life." This life is in the Son of God. But it is not enough to know this; we have to acknowledge we were born with Adam's sin. We have to confess, repent, and then *receive* Jesus into our hearts, and then we have the assurance of eternal life.

How did I miss this? I was twenty-eight years old, and this was the first time I heard this good news! I could not believe that we could *know* we had eternal life. I remember many nights, I would lie in bed and be afraid to close my eyes because "if I died" in my sleep "before I woke," I did not know where I would go for sure. Now here it was written in a book called the Bible "that you may *know* you have eternal life."

As my aunt continued to share these truths with me, I felt an overwhelming peace. I will never forget her face as she spoke so gently, so powerfully, and so humbly. Her face glowed, and her eyes filled with tears of joy. She sobbed as she looked up to the heavens and told Jesus how much she loved Him. She thanked Him over and over for all she had because of Him. I had never seen or heard a love for anyone expressed with such sincerity, humility, and reality. She had a deep abiding faith in a powerful God and a loving Savior. When she prayed, she was simply telling her heavenly Father how much she loved Him, and she thanked Him for His Son, Jesus. Then she prayed for all her family to know Him and receive Him as their Savior. She then prayed for every opportunity to tell everyone about her Jesus, and tell she did. Everywhere she went, everyone she met: on planes, in stores, at the mall. When you met Aunt Mary, she introduced you to Jesus. What an example she was to me. What a glorious time we had together sharing God's love and word.

I knew the Lord had this "last" trip planned for us. God always sends someone at just the right time. My need was great, and He met it through my aunt. I know many others were praying for us too, but it was my Aunt Mary who shared the Gospel with me for the first time. I remember her saying, "When you go home, you need to read your Bible. Look up all of the verses I shared with you and God's Spirit will speak to you. Then you need to receive Jesus into your heart."

I remember thinking, *We do not even own a Bible.* I was twenty-eight years old, and I had never opened the Bible, nor had I ever heard the Gospel message. I know there are many like me. How sad!

Our trip back to Illinois was a long and quiet one, which was very unusual for us. When we were almost home, I recall saying to Bill, "You know, we should really have a family Bible," and he reluctantly nodded. You see, he was raised in a God-fearing, Bible-teaching home. He had wonderful Christian parents who brought him to church and Sunday school every week. He knew the truth—the Gospel—but it was in his head and had not traveled down to his heart. He was running from God. He found out many years later the reason for his rebellion was that he was angry at God.

When Bill was seventeen years old, his twenty-one-year-old brother, who was also his hero, was killed in an automobile accident. This had a great tragic and negative impact on Bill's life. Being a teenager, he could not accept this. He questioned God's fairness and could not understand His sovereignty. "How could this be God's will for my brother?" he asked. That trauma was a turning point for him. His anger turned to rebellion, and he rebelled against the church and all it stood for: his parents, teachers, and all those in authority. He started running from God and was still running fifteen years later. So you can see why he did not want to hear all this "Jesus stuff." He was still angry and was not interested in it for himself. But he felt it was okay if I needed it. I needed it and wanted it too. What happened next was unbelievable! I am convinced that there are no coincidences in the Christian life. Psalm 139 tells us that God had our days planned long before we were born.

The day after we arrived home, there was a knock at my door, and a young man stood there with a smile on his face. I wondered who could be so happy on a Monday morning, and I quickly asked him why he was so happy and what he was selling. He replied, "I am working my way through college and I am selling Bibles. Are you interested?" Can you believe it? I look back and chuckle. God, again, You know what we need and supply it in the most profound way. I gave him a big smile and invited him in. After about thirty minutes, I bought a Bible—the biggest one they had! I bought the one with the words of Jesus printed in red; I didn't want to miss a word! I began reading immediately, and the words just kept popping out of the page, especially John 1:12. I realized I had believed in God and knew that Jesus died on the cross, but had never received Jesus into my heart and life as my Savior. I drank everything in. My heart and mind were open and being filled with the truth. Jesus says in John, "I am the Way, the Truth and the Life. No one can come to the Father except through Me." Oh, how I loved it. This is what I needed. After all those years of searching for happiness in things, I finally found it in Jesus.

In complete brokenness, on October 24, 1968, at ten o'clock in the morning, I was down on my knees by my bed, sobbing and crying out to God, "Oh God," I cried. "I don't even know how to pray, but I know I love You. Forgive me of my sins and come into my heart right now as my Savior and my Lord." At that moment, I was sobbing uncontrollably, but it was like a cleansing, really. As the tears fell out of my eyes, I lifted my head, and I felt the presence of the Lord in me from the top of my head to the bottom of my toes. The whole room was filled with His glory.

There was no question—I was born again. I was saved. I know these terms are overused and abused, but that is what the scriptures say, and it is true. I had found the Truth, and the Truth had set me free. I do not know if it is possible to be humble and proud at the same time, but I am so humbly grateful for God's love, and I am so proud to be a born-again believer in Jesus Christ.

Well, that was a life-changing experience, and when I got up off my knees, that was what I set out to do—change lives. Who do you think I began with? Who do we women think needs the most changing? Yes! Our husbands. I really plead ignorance at this point because I *honestly* did not know any better. I was so excited. I wanted everyone, starting with Bill, to know about my new life. I thought, *This is it!* This is what we had been missing all these years. This was the main piece of our puzzle. I was just *sure* that Bill would agree and receive Christ, and we would all be happy! *Wrong!* He was in no way ready to receive anything, especially from me, and not in the way I was going about it. I came on a little strong, you might say. My experience and excitement was a little overpowering. Bill had two nicknames for me at the time—Susie Spiritual and Sally Self-Righteous. He also said I was "so heavenly *perfect* that I was no earthly good." Yes, I was one of those wives who taped scripture verses on the bathroom mirror, inside the sports page, and put books and tracts with his lunch or briefcase when he traveled. I would read Christian articles to him when we were driving in the car while he was a captive audience. And, oh yes, I dragged him to every Christian couples event unpretentiously.

And guess what? It did not work! In fact, it drove him further away. He really backed off and *would not* respond to anything I had to say, no matter which tactic I used.

Finally, after spending six miserable months trying to change him, I gave up. I prayed and said, "Okay, Lord, I take my hands off! He is Yours and I give him to You, Lord. He is too much for me to handle." It was that "relinquish and surrender all" routine. I got back down on my knees and said, "Lord, *change me*. Show *me* the areas I need to change." That was a release and a relief!

If any of you have husbands who are not Christians, please take your hands off them. Let go and let God work in their lives. He does a much better job. It is our job to love them, accept them, and pray for them. It is God's job to change them. God works in His way and in His time.

I remember well that it did take time—two long years to be exact. During that time, God tried to get Bill's attention, but Bill was not listening. He went through three major hospital stays. A ladder fell on his back and put him in traction, he had an emergency appendectomy, and he suffered a skull fracture with concussion that required surgery. Each time, he would come out of the anesthetic quoting the twenty-third Psalm and saying, "I have got to get right with God." I would be there with my Bible, quoting scripture and praying, saying, "Yes, Bill, yes! This is it! What is it going to take to get you to give up? God is speaking to you. Please listen!"

But he didn't. He went to church for a while and then back to *his* own way again. I reminded myself to pray, trust, and release, to give him to God. I would give Bill over to the Lord one day and take him back the next. It was not easy, but it was the only way to have peace and to survive. During that time, I spent many hours on my knees in prayer and in the Word for hope and encouragement. How I wanted to be a godly wife and a good mother. I spent those six months asking the Lord to change me and take away my habits and old ways in order to help me be the kind of wife and mother He wanted me to be.

The Lord knew what we needed, and He moved us from Rockford, Illinois, to Mt. Prospect in the suburbs of Chicago. My first priority was to find a church we could all attend as a family. We were attending two churches up until then— the Catholic Church on Saturday and the Baptist Church on Sunday. I thought we could do both and blend the two, but of course, it did not work. See, I really felt it was not the church you attended or the religion you practiced, it was what you believed in your heart. What mattered was that Jesus was in your heart as Savior and Lord. Somehow, I had missed it all those years. When I found it, I was so excited, and I wanted everyone to know! I mean, it is really a matter of life and death, isn't it? We either know Jesus is in our hearts and are going to heaven or we are lost and going to hell. Yes, this is the message I wanted to tell, and tell I did. I told everyone: family, friends, strangers, people on the street and in grocery stores, repairmen, bus drivers—everyone. I know I came on a little strong, maybe even a borderline fanatic, in fact; but I did not care. I was as serious as I could be. I was free and wanted everyone to experience this same joy and peace. Well, my family and friends thought I had really gone off the deep end. Looking back, I guess I really did bombard them, but it was because I loved them and wanted to see them in heaven. A good reason, I thought. Again, we have to be careful not to push with our family, but pray first and let the Holy Spirit begin the work. We should be witnesses, but not try to be the Holy Spirit in anyone's life.

I remember the day I finally released that and gave it to God. I made a commitment to love, accept, and pray for people and be a witness to them with my life. These dear ones saw my life changing in such a way that they were drawn to me just as I was drawn to my aunt by her sweet, joyful, and quiet but powerful spirit. People will see Jesus in you through your response to life's circumstances, and then they will listen to you when you verbally witness to them. This is very important in our Christian walk. We may be the only Bible people will see.

Many times, God sends other Christians into our life for us to respect, learn from, and look up to. We see Jesus in them because of their lifestyle and witness. I am so thankful that God provided so many people as examples for me to learn from. At this particular time, He knew what I needed, and He sent to me a dear Christian lady named Golie Robinson. She became one of the three godly women I have dedicated this book to because if it were not for her, I definitely would not be where I am today in my Christian life.

We had moved to Mt. Prospect, and I became involved in a women's Bible study at a church we had visited there, Cumberland Baptist. Many great blessings happened as a result of that visit, and it became our home church. I attended a Saturday seminar for women, and Golie was speaking and singing that day. I felt like I was the only person in that audience. The message seemed to be just for me. Her songs touched my heart in such a way that I felt like I was being filled up with His love and Spirit in me.

One song she sang was "For Those Tears I Died." The lyrics included, "Come to the waters, stand by My side. I know you are thirsty, you won't be denied. I felt every teardrop when in darkness you cried. And I strove to remind you that for those tears I died." I learned something about tears that day. Psalm 56:8 says, "You have seen me tossing and turning through the night. You have collected all my tears and preserved them in your bottle! You have recorded everyone in your book." This was such a revelation to me that my God had such a constant and caring love. He cares enough to collect even my tears and has them in a bottle. He has recorded everyone in His Book. I visualized not just my tears, but the tears of hundreds, thousands, and millions of people. Is He a God who cares? Yes, yes, yes!

I learned many more things from my godsent friend, Golie. She became my spiritual mother. Being a new Christian, I had so much to learn, and I was so hungry for the Word. That is why it means so much to me and why I share it so freely. I *always* go to the scriptures when someone asks me for advice because all of our answers are in God's Word, and it never returns void.

Another important thing I learned from Golie is to always pray before you give advice, asking God to give you wisdom through the power of the Holy Spirit. Afterward, it is important to pray with that person, asking for His confirmation, covering, and blessing. I have to say what I saw in my dear friend that I took to my heart and have tried to live, is a positive, powerful faith and total trust in our Lord Jesus Christ. She also taught me that it is most important to have joy in every circumstance. I know this is not "normal," but it *can* be done, *only*, and I mean *only*, with Jesus's Spirit and power in us. Yes, we can have joy fully in Jesus. God does not expect us to be superficially happy about our circumstances or the world situation, but He wants us to experience the deep, *abiding* joy in our souls when we are totally surrendered to His will for our lives. We can claim Galatians 2:20, "I am crucified *in* Christ that no longer I live, but He lives in me. This life I now live, I live by faith in the Son of God" (emphasis added). When you find your identity in Christ, you will be free. Free from the power of fear, worry, guilt, and all of the barriers and bondage that keep us from living the victorious Christian life. These truths are found throughout the scriptures and written by many authors such as Watchman Nee, Hannah Whitehall Smith, Hudson Taylor, and many others. This is the "exchanged life" as we know it today—Jesus living His life in us through the Holy Spirit.

Golie also taught me how to live joyfully with an unsaved husband as she did, and still experienced great peace and joy. She loved her husband with an agape love, sacrificially and unconditionally, as Jesus tells us to do. After God, her husband was first in her life, and she was always careful to seek his permission to speak and sing at seminars. She was sensitive to never interfere with his schedule. His needs came first. This was not being a doormat, but being lovingly obedient to God and submissive to her husband, and she was blessed for it.

I was learning to take my hands off Bill and trying not to manipulate or control him, but to only love and accept him. This was not easy, and I could not do it in my own strength. But the Spirit of God in me could and did, when I let go and let God.

I remember almost *every* day I would call and ask Golie to pray for me. "I'm doing it again," I would tell her. She would say, "Jean, you just gave it to the Lord yesterday—don't take it back today. Leave it at the cross." I know from experience that this is the hardest thing to do for all of us. But I also know it *can* be done. If I can do it, you can! Each time, it becomes a little easier and more time in between. Less of self and more of Christ. We need to realize that Jesus Christ is our source of strength and peace, and He *is all* we need.

When we can come to this point in our lives, it frees us up and takes a great burden off our husbands. They just *cannot* meet all of our needs. Mrs. Billy Graham said, "Don't expect your husband to be what only Jesus Christ can be in your life." This is so true. When we turn to Him, receive Him, and trust Him, we *will* be content in who we are in Him and not expect our husbands, children, or anyone else to be what only Jesus Christ can be in our lives.

A note of encouragement for singles: God does have the best plan for your life too. It may be to marry someday, or it may be to remain single. Each state is a gift from God. As the Bible says in 1 Corinthians 7:7, "God gives some the gift of a husband and others He gives the gift of being able to stay happily unmarried."

When I quote that verse to married women, some of them exclaim, "My husband—a gift? Can I return or exchange him? How about a refund?" No! Seriously, if we would all realize that our circumstances—married or being single—are a gift from God, we would look at them in a different light and be able to accept them as God's gift for us.

Another confirmation and encouragement for singles is found in verse 34, "A girl who is not married is busy with the Lord's work. She wants to please Him in all that she does." Verse 38 says, "So the person who is married does well, and the person who does not marry does even better." Again, God's will and plan for each of us is best.

This is my prayer for every woman single or married: stop expecting any other person or source to meet your needs. Receive from Jesus all that He has for you. In Jesus, we have everything: life, hope, joy, peace, comfort, and care. Our needs are met. "My God shall supply *all* your needs" (Phil. 4:19). We can be the woman, wife, mother, and friend God wants us to be. Christ *in* us is all we need! We *can* do all things through Christ Who gives us the strength. Oh, what joy to walk fully in His strength and power! This gave me the utmost peace and the security I needed. It truly was the stepping-stone to a closer, more intimate relationship with my Lord. My foundation in Him was becoming strong, secure, and firm through His Word, and by believing and claiming His promises. I focused on Jesus as my ultimate "need-meeter."

> Jesus, You Are All I Need
> By Jean Bufton (May, 1993)

>> Jesus, Jesus, You are all I need,
>> Your life is enough, yes indeed.
>> Forgive me for looking in other places,
>> Trying to find on their faces,
>> Acceptance, understanding, and care,
>> When You alone are always there.
>> Your love for me is steadfast and true,
>> Your Word tells me what to do.
>> We all need people and a good Friend.
>> But it's Your love that will never end.
>> We look to others for peace of mind,
>> Even though they are helpful and kind,
>> And with their prayers they do intercede,
>> Jesus, You alone will meet my need.
>> As I lay my burdens at the cross,
>> Yes, I will experience some loss.
>> This is our old self, the flesh, you know.
>> What a relief to finally let go.
>> Letting Christ live in me,
>> And be completely free.
>> What peace we experience, you will see,
>> When we surrender our stubborn will,
>> Then and only then our hearts can be still.

HOPE FOR THE DAYS AHEAD

As we come before the throne of grace,
And stay prayerfully in that quiet place,
You can speak to us and show us the way,
Guiding us through each and every day.
Then when our foundation in You is secure,
All of life's trials, we can endure.
Our battles will finally be won,
We'll marvel at what You have done.
You've said, "My grace is sufficient
In your time of need,
Along the best pathway I will lead.
Trust in Me and you will see,
In Jesus, there is complete victory."

Chapter 3

S---------:
Ugh! That Dreaded Word!

At this point in my life, the word "submission" was not even in my vocabulary. I did not even know how to spell it, nor did I want to learn how. No wonder I was having such a hard time releasing this area to the Lord. I did not know the true meaning of the word. I just remember thinking that if I cannot change my husband, I'll concentrate on my children. I did want to be a good mother and raise them in a godly way. God knew what I needed and had a plan for me.

A few of the women from our church were going to a retreat and asked me to go. I had never been to a weekend retreat before, so I agreed to attend with them. The topic was God's Plan for the Family—just what I needed! I'll never forget that first session. My seat was in front, in the middle of a pew with the ladies from our church on either side of me. I said, "Okay, Lord, I'm ready to hear now how to be a good, godly mother." Well, when the speaker introduced herself, she told us that she was single. That sent up a red flag for me because I wondered how she was going to teach us how to be a good mother when she could not even understand or relate to what we were going through? She was the Dean of Women at a college, so I thought, *Hmm*. She must have some credibility. I relaxed a little and listened. She said the retreat would focus on being a godly woman, wife, and mother, and that we would learn God's plan and order for these roles.

First, of course, was being a godly woman, and I knew I needed to learn more about that. Then she said we would be learning about the wife's role, especially in the area of *submission. Oh no*! I thought. Not submission! Not that dreaded word. I could not even relate to it, and besides, how in the world was she going to teach us a lesson on submission when she wasn't even married? *Oh brother*, I thought. *What have I gotten myself into*? Honestly, if I had not been down in front in the middle of the pew, I really believe I would have left during that first session. But God knew where I needed to be, and He had placed me there, tucked me in between all those women. So I said, "Okay, Lord. *I'll sit here and listen if You really want me to.*" At that point, I did say, "I'll open my ears and my heart, and I will receive what You have to say through this servant of Yours." Again, here was that surrender of *my* will.

Well, much to my surprise and amazement, this dear lady was a fabulous speaker. Her name was Verna Berky, and the seminar was called Enriched Living. Because she was single and did not have the responsibility of a family, she could go every weekend all over the country and share these truths, the truth of God's Word. Everything she said was based on scripture and God's plan for the family. She used illustrations and practical applications from women who attended the seminars and found outstanding results. Step-by-step, word-by-word, and scripture-by-scripture, I learned for the first time the true meaning of submission.

I also learned what submission is *not*. It is *not* being a doormat where the husband is so dominant and controlling that his

S---------: UGH! THAT DREADED WORD!

words and actions strip you of all your self-worth, which gives the feeling of being stepped on emotionally. Submission is *not* him lording over you as in a master-slave position. Especially in an abusive situation, I do not believe women should stay in a harmful circumstance such as this for her sake and her children's. This is not the submission God is talking about, and one should seek help and counsel if this is the case. On the other hand, it is not being so submissive that you refuse to take responsibility or have an opinion and use that as an excuse, then live as a martyr, full of self-pity with the "oh, poor me" syndrome. No, submission is none of these.

Here is how the Bible defines submission. In Ephesians 5:21, it says, "Be subject to one another out of reverence for Christ." Verse 22 states, "Wives, be subject to your husbands as to the Lord." Submission is the way we express love toward one another out of reverence for Christ. I must admit, this made it much easier for me as I went on to see God's plan for the family.

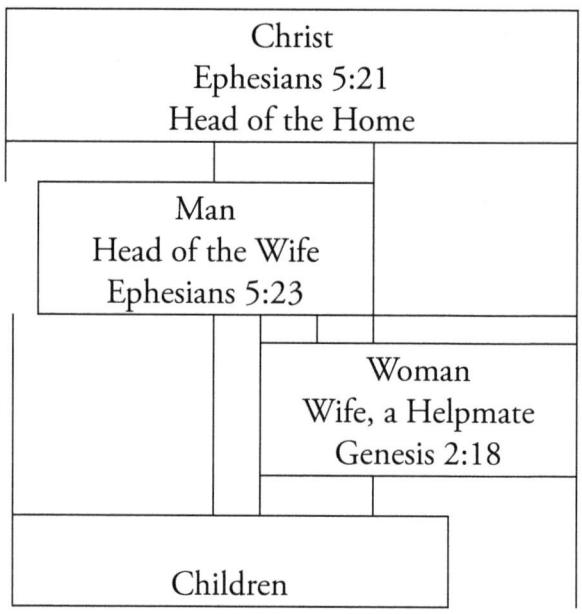

In this diagram, you see Christ as the Head, then the man under Christ as the head of the wife. The woman is under Christ and alongside as a helpmate to her husband, and the children are under both of them.

I once heard that when God created woman, He did not take a bone from Adam's foot so he could step on her. Nor did He take a bone from his head so he could lord over her. He took a rib from his side close to his heart so he could protect her, and they could be side-by-side partners—with her as his helpmate to complete God's plan for the family!

When we think of submission, we need to think of Christ first, remembering His example of submission on the cross. The Bible tells us in Philippians 2:5 that our "attitude" should be the kind that was shown to us by Jesus. He humbled Himself and became a servant. The Bible also says in Ephesians 4:23 how our *attitude* and thoughts should be changing for the better. I really see submission as an *attitude* first and an action second. When we change our attitude about it, only *then* can we be submissive as we are unto the Lord. Only then can we *choose* to put another person's needs, desires, and rights ahead of ours.

It became so clear to me, and I remember thinking, *Yes, I do want to do what God wants me to do*. In obedience to Christ and in order to do that, I had to change my attitude about submission. I knew I could not do it on my own (none of us can). At that moment, I said, "Okay. I surrender this attitude to You, Lord. Fill me with Your strength and power, and give me a servant's attitude to be submissive to my husband." Remember now, the old self did not want to, but Christ in me did. When I did surrender all, I had a whole new perception of my attitude, words, and actions. When we put it in perspective, when we are first submissive as unto the Lord, it is easier to be submissive to our husbands.

S---------: UGH! THAT DREADED WORD!

Remember also in the last chapter, I talked about making a choice. We do need to *choose* to do this even if we do not feel like it. It is an act of our will. I made this choice. I honored Christ, and the feelings *did* come later.

This did not happen overnight. It is a process, but it does work. Each day, we must remember Christ's example to us in laying aside His "rights." As it says in Philippians 2:6,7, "Jesus—who was God—did not demand and cling to His rights as God, but laid aside His mighty power and humbled Himself and became a servant in obedience to God." This truth became a reality to me, and I was humbled in the sight of the Lord. At that seminar, I learned to give up my rights in every area of my life, especially in the area of my husband. It was my job to love him as Christ loved me, sacrificially and unconditionally. It was not my job to change him. That was God's job. By yielding my rights to these areas of control, it took away the frustration and fighting. What freedom I felt as this burden was lifted.

I remember I came home and wrote a letter to Bill, telling him what I had done and asking for his forgiveness in the areas I had been trying to take charge in. I even asked him to make me a list of the things I did that irritated him and ways that I could change for the better. Needless to say, he was shocked, and he staggered in disbelief. He was sure this was just some weird stage I was in. He never thought it would last, but it did. He said he wanted to stay around just to see how long it would last! Actually, it was God working through me that was giving Bill hope for us. I learned that we cannot change anyone else. If I wanted change in my home, it *had* to start with *me*, and change I did. Not only in my role as a wife, but also as a mother.

The topic of the second half of the retreat was how to be a godly mother. I really needed help in that area as I wanted our children to not only know Jesus as their Savior, but also know Him as a loving Father—one who disciplines because He loves us. As it says in Hebrews 12:6, "For the Lord corrects and disciplines everyone He loves." Verse 11 reads, "At the time, discipline does not bring joy, but afterward it produces peaceful fruit." That is what I wanted to see happen with my children, so I listened intently to all that was said and took notes on how to apply these biblical principles in a godly way. I realized I was not handling my discipline in the right way and knew I needed to change. I needed to project the loving discipline of the Lord, not the "do it now" or "because I say so" routine. My tone of voice, countenance, and facial expressions needed to characterize what Christ would do in the same situation. I know that sounds almost impossible to do, and it is left to our own resources, old ways, and "spontaneous spoons" (wood or Teflon). But I am here to say it is *never* too late.

Our children were ages seven, nine, and eleven at the time and just about ready to go into the terrible teens. They were fast approaching the smart-mouth stage. Something had to be done quickly! I remember the night I was leaving for this retreat. The kids were in a typical scene of arguing back and forth: "It's your fault." "No, it's your fault"—which is not unusual when you are ready to go to some Christian event. Instead of losing my cool and threatening with the Teflon spoon (my rod), I laughed and said, "Stop! I do not want you to hurt yourselves before I get back. I am going to a seminar to learn how to handle this the right way!" And learn I did!

I learned what God wanted me to do as a Christian mother. It was to love them and discipline them as He does for us. Proverbs 3:12 says, "For whom the Lord loves, He corrects even as a father corrects his son in whom he delights." I quoted this scripture to the kids the day I returned.

They were not too impressed.

S---------: UGH! THAT DREADED WORD!

Actually, they looked wide-eyed at me in amazement! I had "laid down my spoon" and had taken up the sword of the Spirit, which is the Word of God. They could tell I was serious, but with a different attitude. There it is again—*that attitude*. What a difference a day makes! I continued with a Christ-like calm attitude, and went a step further to humble myself before them and asked them to forgive me for the way I had been disciplining them because it was not done in a godly way. Yelling, screaming, and breaking the spoon on the kitchen counter was not the way God would have me do it. I bowed my head, we all held hands, and I prayed. I prayed for strength, courage, commitment, cooperation, change in spirit and attitude; and I prayed for each of them as well. I convinced them that with God's help, I was going to discipline them with the firm but loving discipline of the Lord. I was not going to "spare the rod and spoil the child," but it would be loving correction. They knew I was serious, and they respected my stand as I began to retrain myself to train up my children in the way they should go—God's way. It was not easy, but it did work.

Slowly, steadily, and *very* consistently, we had some major changes and real breakthroughs. When I did discipline them, I always told them I loved them; and afterward, I prayed with them. It was not always well received at the time, but I know those were the times when our foundation of respect became stronger as they related love with discipline and discipline with love. Revelation 3:19 says, "To those whom I dearly love, I discipline."

We asked our oldest son to write his thoughts on our way of discipline, and this was what Bill said:

> "I remember being disciplined many times, but I know that there was never a time when I didn't deserve it. I was treated fairly while I

was younger, and one of the most important ways that I learned to grow up was through discipline and love, or as I put it—discipline with love. This is a great way for parents to make it with their kids—to be loving, consistent, and fair. When parents tell their kids they will be punished, they should follow through with it and be fair with their punishment, which should occur at the time of the incident. My parents are cool. I mean, when I was growing up, it wasn't roses all the time, but they are winners. They disciplined with love many times, and treated us fairly and with respect."

During that time, the children and I bonded together in prayer for Bill, their dad, to receive the Lord; and soon after that, he did. In fact, Bill was amazed at the change in me and the way I handled things: him, the children, the home, and responsibilities in general. He began to soften and even came to church with us. The story of Bill's conversion is so incredible and again, truly a testimony to God's faithfulness and answer to many prayers.

Bill used to say, "Behind every good man, there is a woman pushing." Now he says, "Behind every good man, there is a woman praying," and pray I did! I had everyone I knew praying for Bill—he didn't have a chance! There is a great book by Evelyn Christianson called *What Happens When Women Pray*. I will tell you what happens: God hears and answers! Yes, when I stood aside, stopped pushing, and started praying, God began to work, and much faster with me out of the way.

I do not know why we women think we can help God with our husbands. Be assured—He does *not* need our help at *all!*

S---------: UGH! THAT DREADED WORD!

He *does* a much better job on His own and in His own timing. Remember, it is our job to love him and God's job to change him! I know it seems so long sometimes, but God's timing is perfect.

We were pretty well settled in at Cumberland Baptist Church in Mt. Prospect, Illinois. To be honest, Bill was drawn in by the men's basketball team, led by Phil Gustafson. He and his wife, Barbara, took us under their wing and are dear friends to this day. How I thank God for Christian sports programs at churches. Bill loved sports, and these men ministered to him in such a comfortable, casual way. It was not pushy or preachy, just acceptance and love. We began to do social things with them also. This was such a nice switch from the business world activities we had to be a part of at times. We enjoyed many evenings of fun and fellowship with the wives after the basketball games.

I remember one Saturday evening after a game, we stopped for pizza. The men were discussing the coming week's events at church. They were having a special speaker starting on Sunday morning and continuing on every night during the week. I could see Bill rolling his eyes and saying, "Well, I will go on Sunday morning, but you can be sure I am not going every night through the rest of the week, especially not Monday, because I never give up watching Monday Night Football for anything."

At this point in Bill's life, I was thankful he was even going on Sunday morning, let alone all week long. Bill was flying high in the business world at this time in our lives. He was in a partnership in an aerospace manufacturing company, and they called themselves the Dynamic Duo. Bill handled all the outside public relations and sales, and his partner handled the inside production responsibilities. Bill was into the success syndrome, which was based on performance, income, dollars, big cars, big houses, expensive clothes, jewelry, trips, and all of the added luxuries that went along with that type of lifestyle. It was totally contrary to what I wanted, needed, or even agreed with. But I went along with it, and I never gave up hope. The more I took my hands off, prayed, and trusted the Lord, the more I could see God working.

Early in my Christian life, I took Romans 8:28 for my life verse: "And we know that in all things, God works for the good of those who love Him, who have been called according to His purpose." I remember thinking many times, *All things, Lord? Really? Even this?* And He would seem to gently say, "Yes, even this! I will work together for your good and My glory." As I waited, prayed, and trusted God, I could see that happening right before me. As long as I kept my eyes on the Lord, I was okay; but if my focus got on me or my circumstances, I would lose sight of the ultimate victory. So I continued to let go and let God work "all things together for His glory."

I will never forget that Sunday morning when we were frantically getting ready for church. Doesn't Satan have a heyday on Sunday mornings? We were running late as usual with three kids fighting and trying to find a shoe, belt, or barrette. When we finally got in the car, we were all upset: Bill at me, me at the kids, and the kids at each other. What a trap we fell into, arguing as we pulled up to the church. It was now 10:55 a.m., and the lot was full because of the special speaker. So we had to park pretty far away and walk a long distance. This made it eleven o'clock, and the music had already started to play. The ushers saw us coming, a family of five, and they looked hurriedly for seats for us. It was a typical Baptist church, and the pews in the back filled up first. In fact, even the extra chairs they had set up were full, but the first pew up in front always seems to be available. No one wants to be *that* close, and we didn't either. But as luck (the Lord) would have it, there was a very friendly and excited usher up front motioning to us to come and sit up there. By then, it was 11:05 a.m., and the choir had just finished singing. The congregation was starting to turn around and see who was back there waiting to be seated. So very reluctantly, with our big super-saint, superficial smiles on our faces, we paraded down that long aisle. Heads turned to watch as this family of five, trying but to no avail to be inconspicuous, was seated.

Well, there we were in the front row. Little did I know *then* that this was exactly where God wanted us to be. Oh, did He have a plan for that day! And yes, all things were working together for good, even being late was for good that day. If we had been early and had sat in the back, Bill could have slipped out early. But God wanted Bill's complete attention up front, and He had it because when the speaker, Jim Counihan, began preaching, he seemed to direct his attention to the front row. Jim is left-handed, and we were on the left side. He began his message this way, "Do you know that God loves you just the way you are?" His eyes and gestures pointed right at Bill. I could not believe it! I thought Bill would have been uncomfortable, but he was smiling and liked the fact that God "loved him just the way he was."

In the next breath, Jim finished that statement with, "But too much to leave you that way." I could see Bill's face as his mind was receiving these profound thoughts: "God loves you just the way you are, *but* too much to leave you that way!" That hit him right between the eyes, and I could sense Bill getting a little uncomfortable. The preacher/evangelist went on to tell his story and gave his message. It was so appropriate for Bill that you would have thought I had briefed Jim for three days, but alas, I could not take credit for it. I sat in that pew praising the Lord and holding back the tears of joy. Honestly, if there had not been one other person in that church that day, I felt God would have sent him specifically for Bill. The message was perfect! Thank you, Lord!

Jim was a man's man, had been in the world, a bartender in Las Vegas, in the Navy, and doing his own thing for years. Then, at the age of twenty-four, he was introduced to the person of Jesus Christ. His life was miraculously transformed when he received Christ into his life. He went to college and seminary at the age of twenty-six and was now an evangelist giving New Life Conferences at churches throughout the country. Jim was from Minnesota and at that time was the president of the American Evangelism Association.

Again, I claim Psalm 139. You will hear me reference this many times throughout my book because it is so significant and important. Verse 16 tells us that our days were planned even before we were born, and He has them recorded in His Book. God knew Bill would be in that church that day in that front pew, listening to a speaker he could relate to so well. He also knew all about the events that were about to happen.

At the end of the message, I could see Bill's heart had been touched, and the Holy Spirit was working. Pastor Jim was ready to give an invitation to come forward and receive Christ. Bill swore that he was *never* going to walk down an aisle in a church (how convenient, Lord, that we were guided to the front of the church so he did not have to!) See, even that too was planned by God. When it was time to come forward and make a commitment to Christ, Bill had to take only <u>one</u> step (actually, it was sideways). And he *did*!

On that day in September of 1971, Bill received Christ as his Savior and turned his life over to Him. I stood by his side, and together we gave everything to Him—all on the altar. We gave our lives, our children, our time, our talents, our business, our belongings, our finances—*everything*! What a day that was for us! The beginning of a whole new life. God did it! He answered my prayers and the prayers of so many at just the right

S---------: UGH! THAT DREADED WORD!

time—His! Remember, let go and let God do it! His timing is best.

We look back now and laugh as Bill tells the story of how he *did* go Sunday night, Monday night, Tuesday night, Wednesday night, and all through the week. In fact, on Monday night, he said to the preacher, "I even gave up Howard Cosell for you! That is something I would never do." The Lord had already begun to do an incredible work in him.

The essence of the meeting was training us to share our faith, to witness one-on-one. How exciting that by Friday, we were ready to go out calling on people who had visited our church. We had to pick a partner, and Bill did not want to go with me, so he picked our pastor, Bob Hails, thinking he would do all of the talking since Bill was such a new Christian. But oh, our pastor was so wise and definitely led by God. He and Bill went out together and had two calls to make. The pastor told Bill he would take the first call, and Bill was relieved when no one was home, sure that the pastor would take the second one too. But no, the pastor told Bill, "This one is yours." Bill said he remembered praying as he went up the walk, "Oh Lord, please don't let anyone be home!" But God had that planned too.

At home was a woman who had not been to church for a long time. She explained she had a lot of habits and excuses, all of which Bill could relate to.

It is so great to see that God uses each of us just as we are and where we are in our Christian life to relate to people. Bill needed to share with this woman because they had so much in common. He could understand where she was coming from. Before the hour was up, the three were kneeling before her coffee table, praying as she received Christ as her Savior. What a mountaintop experience that was for Bill. God's timing, yes, as within six months, that dear lady contracted cancer and went home to be with her Lord. Bill looks forward to her greeting him "when we all get to heaven." Truly, what a day of rejoicing that will be! Bill learned a great lesson that day—it is not our ability God wants, it is our *availability* to Him. He then gives us the ability to speak, witness, and serve.

That week, our new life in Christ together began! Pastor Jim asked Bill to join him at several more crusades in South Dakota and Canada. He wanted Bill to share his testimony. Pastor Jim watched as God used Bill to relate to so many businessmen, young people, and married couples. God was definitely calling Bill into the ministry. Jim not only became his brother in the Lord, but his mentor and close friend even to this day, along with our families. Thank you Lord for bringing another Godly person to guide us as we grew in the Lord. Bill grew by leaps and bounds, and of course, the "things of the world were growing strangely dim" and becoming less important.

As could be expected, this change in Bill's life had a definite effect on his business relationships. The kids, my prayer partners, and I had been praying about that for quite a while because his job was consuming most of Bill's time, thoughts, and energies. We wanted Bill with us totally: in spirit, soul, and body. We knew it may mean giving up a lot, but we were ready to make any sacrifice. Bill was feeling the pressure too as he could not live two lives anymore and did not want to continue in the business partnership. He felt like he had become unequally yoked with a non-Christian. We had agreed that he would give notice on December 15 and be done by the end of that year.

One Wednesday night, just two weeks before Christmas, I was at church and Bill slipped in alongside of me. They were having a short time for prayer requests, and Bill raised his hand. He said, "I have one. I just quit my job." He looked at me and I smiled. I knew it would be soon, and this was a little sooner than I had expected. But I had a deep peace in my spirit know-

S---------: UGH! THAT DREADED WORD!

ing it was the *right* thing to do and knowing that God would provide and take care of us. Deuteronomy 31:7–8 says, "Be strong and courageous—be not afraid. I will be with you. I will not forsake you. Your God is with you wherever you go." This was His promise, and we claimed it for our lives and future.

What could have been the bleakest Christmas ever with no job, no prospects, tons of bills and payments, turned out to be the best! We had great faith, and we knew we were right where God wanted us—at the end of ourselves. Not trusting in a job, a paycheck, or a prospect, but totally *in Him*. With that step of faith, we began a new life. Bill had to give up his company car, a gold Cadillac, and all of the other luxuries and amenities he had like expense accounts, trips, tax write-offs, and Christmas bonuses.

Bill remembers well driving around that winter in our 1965 car and the heater going out on the freeway. A humbling experience, yes, but oh so right—to be in the center of God's will. As we prayed for direction, He gave us this confirmation in His Word in Psalm 32:8, "'I will instruct you,'" says the Lord, 'and guide you along the best pathway for your life. I will advise you and watch your progress.'" He did guide us and direct us to start our own business in our home, a manufacturer's representative business. This could be done with no overhead and a minimal investment. Our investment was a red card table and one piece of equipment, a manual typewriter. God did watch our progress. In fact, it progressed so well that by the following year, Bill opened his own manufacturing company called Tri-State Manufacturing. Yes, with that first step of faith on our part, God did part the sea, and He blessed us. He did more than we could ever ask or think as it says in Ephesians 3:20—infinitely beyond our highest prayers, desires, thoughts, or hopes. Yes, He gave us *Hope for the Days Ahead*!

Chapter 4

Hang On! We're Headed for Happiness!

Bill and I had moved our family around a lot—about six times in ten years. We had settled into a lovely tri-level home in the suburbs of Chicago in Mt. Prospect. After all these years of move after move, we finally finished decorating our dream home. The drapes, furniture, and wall coverings were a decorator's dream. The living room was the perfect shade of light blue with a matching light blue velvet sofa and crystal chandeliers. The windows were adorned with Austrian pouf sheers and antique satin drapes—gorgeous! I chose a silver-white dining room set and matching end tables, and completed the look with new carpeting. I had just hung the last picture on the wall and the last accessory piece graced the end table—perfect! Every room was complete! We improved this already large home with an added-on game room, a spacious family room, new pool in the backyard, and a finished basement.

Needless to say, we were pretty well settled in that home, neighborhood, and church. We felt nice and secure, ministering, loving the pastor, people, and our surroundings. The business was flourishing, and everything seemed to be going very well. Some of you know what happens when we get in the "contented and secure" state. Yes, God sometimes has another plan and place for you, as He well did for us. I was not only teaching a Bible study, but Bill and I had a young married couples' class in our home on Sunday nights, which was also growing. We were leading mini-retreats, teaching the junior high group; Bill was an elder, and I was on the Christian education board. Yes, we *were* busy. We also were taking a night class at Moody Bible Institute on marriage and the family. We really had a concern for young couples who were struggling in their marriages like Bill and I had for so long. Our concern turned into a burden, and our burden to a commitment to go back to school and prepare for some type of family ministry. Remember now, we were thirty-six and thirty-eight years old, had three teenagers, a thriving manufacturing business, and a sizable home. With our ministry at the church, we really had enough going for us.

However, we felt this nudge from God. His still, small voice was saying, "Go!" Mind you, these were not hastily made decisions. In fact, we began by praying and searching the scriptures. Psalm 25:4–5a states, "Show me the path where I should go, oh Lord. Point out the right road for me to walk. Lead me, teach me." Psalm 73:22–24 states, "You are holding my hand. You will keep on guiding me all my life, with Your wisdom and counsel." That was the next step. We did seek counsel from godly men. We did want His will for our lives, and this was a tremendous decision.

During that year, we had purchased a small cottage in Winona Lake, Indiana. It was a great place to get away from our busy schedule, the pressure of work, and the pace of the city. It was a quiet retreat and a recreational place to go on the weekends. Winona Lake is noted for two things—its Christian conference grounds and Grace College and Seminary. Well-known speakers come for a week at a time during the summer.

The population of 2,800 expands to about ten thousand during these conferences. It was the home of Billy Sunday, the famous evangelist. We really loved our weekends there; and the kids enjoyed the lake, basketball camps, and the Youth for Christ conferences. We enjoyed watching the kids and attending various conferences ourselves. We got to know quite a few people at Grace College, so we sought the advice and counsel of pastors, professors, and friends. We felt God was leading us to go back to college to prepare for the ministry. We did not know exactly how, what, or where; but we knew we had to learn more before we could continue teaching.

I will never forget telling our pastor and the people in our home church to pray about our decision. They were shocked and unhappy at the prospect of losing us. As I said, our lives revolved around the church, its people, and our ministry there. We sought the Lord for a year, and by the following spring, things were looking pretty good. Doors were opening for us to move to Winona Lake, and we felt God leading.

I will never forget a rainy day in March when I was sitting in my lovely light-blue dining room, teaching a Bible lesson on submission. Remember when that word wasn't even in my vocabulary? Here I was, teaching other women how to be submissive to their husbands. God really has a sense of humor! The following is a hilarious story and great lesson I had to learn in letting go, taking my hands off the house, and being submissive to my husband.

Bill was in Winona Lake that day looking for some rental property to buy to supplement our income while we were in school. We anticipated enrolling for the fall semester. Our house was for sale, and steps were being taken to prepare for this move. I chuckle when I think back on that day because I should have known. Every time you commit to teach on a certain subject, you are usually tested on it. This makes for a good lesson application and wonderful illustration. With that in mind, back to my dining room.

Bill called me from Winona Lake right as we were beginning to pray. I went to the phone and asked if he had found some rental property to supplement our income. He answered, "No, but I *did* find our house!"

"Our house?" I exclaimed, trying to remain composed. With a forced smile on my face and with all of the Bible-study ladies watching, I said, "What do you mean you picked out our house? Do you mean the one we will be living in?"

"Yes!" he said confidently.

In my mind, I was thinking, *How could he? Oh, he wouldn't, would he? Did he really pick out our house without my approval or "godly advice," or even my opinion?* Really, I couldn't believe what I was hearing. Very timidly, and still smiling, I said, "Oh, really? What is it like?" As soon as I asked that, I knew I was in for the biggest lesson in submission I had ever had. He started to explain that the house was cedar and wood, had a real rustic look, and was just perfect. *Oh great!* I thought. *Perfect for whom? A hermit in the woods maybe, but not me!* Here I was, standing in the dining room, looking at all that beautiful light blue furniture that I had waited so long for thinking how out of place it would be in a rustic cedar and wood house. I looked into the faces of my friends as they were sitting on my gorgeous, off-white ornate dining room chairs with the velvet seats, being served from my Gorham china and silver. I knew they were waiting anxiously for me to share my news.

I quickly told Bill, still with that frozen smile on my face, "Honey, I think we'd better talk more about this when you get home. Hurry now, but drive carefully. We will be praying for you." I hung up the phone and told my friends, "Oh my. You need to pray for me!" As we began to pray, I confided in them my suspicion that this was about to become a lesson, the biggest lesson in submission I had ever had. It was! It was a good thing I did not know at the time just how much.

Bill came home that night, and bless his heart, he was so excited. I was trying to be, but the more he told me about the house, the more of a sickening feeling I got in my stomach. "Will *any* of our furniture fit in *that* house?" I asked. Bill looked around and thought.

Finally, he answered, "*No*, I don't think so, but we can sell all of this 'stuff' with the house and start over!"

Start over, I thought. *Again?* Hadn't I done that six times already? I had just gotten everything here just how I liked it (perfect!) and now he was ready to leave it all and just start over? I really had to go before the Lord with this one. I had to reevaluate my priorities and thoughts. Did I feel the Lord was leading us? Yes, that had been confirmed in so many ways. Did I know He had the best plan for our lives? Oh, yes. I read just recently in Isaiah 55:8, "This plan of Mine is not what you would work out. Neither are My thoughts the same as yours."

Okay, Lord, I thought. *I accept that You must have the best and only plan for us.* I had to search my soul and ask myself if I was hanging on to *my* house and *my* things. I didn't think so, but I soon learned that maybe, just maybe, they meant more to me than I wanted to admit.

Well, as Bill and I continued to talk that night, we decided to drive to Winona Lake the next day so I could see the house Bill had chosen. In the back of my mind, I was thinking that if I *really* didn't like it, we could get out of the deal. I did not know that Bill had already given them a check to hold the house. *I was trying* to be somewhat submissive and go there with an open mind.

We left the next day; and it was a dreary, rainy, cold day. The drive down was a very quiet one. We could not even enjoy the scenery because of the rain and the cloudy skies. We actually never went to Winona Lake in the winter or early spring, so my only impression of beautiful Winona Lake was driving down in the sunny summer when everything was in bloom. At that time, there were weeping willows blowing gently in the warm breeze from the lake and the sun glistening across the water like glass. Boats sailed leisurely by, children swam, older people sat relaxing on the benches, feeding the ducks, and people walked around the lake while waiting for the next conference to begin. The Christian bookstore played hymns all day and was a favorite spot. The Lamp, which was the only cafe in town, filled with happy people eating and meeting from all over the world. It was a perfect haven of rest and relaxation—Little Jerusalem, they called it.

Those thoughts were going through my mind. Memories of the Winona Lake I remembered from our summer weekends there. Never for a moment did I even consider that the town closed up for the winter and that it got cold and rainy. I did not think about how the leaves fell from the trees in the winter, stark and shivering in the cold. Winona Lake was our summer sanctuary, and I *was* looking forward to moving there. Oh yes! Reality set in as we were driving down Route 30. *We are moving there soon, and we are on our way to see our new house*, I thought. Suddenly, the summer sun had set and the cold winter weather had left its mark. A shiver ran through me as we entered Winona Lake this day.

Now before I go on, I need to mention three things—three things that are very significant for you to remember as I continue my story. I am scared to death of water, and I do not swim. I get motion sickness *very* easily, even when I watch a boat in the water or on television. Last, but certainly not least, my *least* favorite color was green. Remember, my whole house was decorated in light blue. We blue lovers usually do not like green, and I didn't! With those things in mind, let's continue our trip to Winona Lake.

As we entered the town on this cold March day, I was surprised that the bright, sun-shiny little town with all of the people had turned into a cold, drab, barren almost ghost town. All of the summer cottages were closed up. No one was feeding the ducks. The lake was turbulent with rising waves splashing against the shore. The willow trees looked bare and lifeless. Only a few people were in the usually crowded bookstore. The conference grounds were deserted. I looked around and thought, *Where is everyone? Whom will I talk to? Oh my, what has happened to our wonderful Winona Lake?* I have noticed that it has taken me many words to describe Winona Lake. I recall that when we brought Florence Littauer there to speak, she described it in *one* word, which is very unlike Florence. Her description was "*gray*"! Are you getting the picture? Now that I have set the scene, let's proceed through town to our house.

We drove down Winona Avenue and turned right on Administration Boulevard which curves around the lake and turns into Auditorium Boulevard. This particular piece of land is called the Island because there is a small channel that goes through, something like Balboa Island, California. Well, not quite. Anyway, as we approached the curve and it changed to Auditorium, we slowed down and stopped in front of this two-story, square, *green* cedar house with a flat roof. It was nestled one foot between two closed-up cottages. There were no neighbors in the winter, but oh my, in the summer we were so close, we could reach out our side windows and pass things back and forth. As I looked up out of the corner of my eye, I gasped! Bill said, "Well, *this is it*, our house!" I went into shock for a split second, thinking that this was some sort of a joke or a nightmare. But again, with my mind whirling as fast as my mouth does, I immediately had my bucket of paint out and was visually painting the house (light blue). You know, we women can repaint and redecorate in an instant if we have to, and I had to!

Well, as I reluctantly got out of the car and went up to the door, this sweet lady greeted us with a big smile and could not wait to show us "our house."

As the door swung open, my eyes went to the carpet—it was green. The wood walls were a tint of green. The accessories were gold and green, very tastefully done, but a far cry from my blue, velvet, and crystal chandeliers.

At the end of the *narrow* hall, I stood at the kitchen counter and looked wide-eyed in amazement as the kitchen looked out through the *small* family room to a long, narrow sun porch with fourteen windows. And what do you suppose was thirty feet out our back door? Yes, the lake! Now we don't like yard work, but who wanted one thousand acres of Winona Lake in our backyard?

At that moment, the wind started to blow harder, and the waves were whipping up over the sea wall. I felt like I was in Noah's Ark! The rain was hitting all fourteen windows, making little tiny spots all over. May I say here that I am one of those clean fanatics? In fact, I *love* to clean bathrooms. Honest, I do! *Why?* Because I cannot stand water spots, and here were all those water spots forming on the windows. *Oh no*, I thought, and my mind was racing now. I was thinking about our future in this house. I visualized my three kids out in the lake, thirty feet from our back door, drowning, and I can't save them because I do not know how to swim. Besides, I'm in here with motion sickness, trying to get these water spots off the windows while frustratingly trying to adjust to all this green! It was like having your whole life pass before your eyes in a split second.

Before my thoughts progressed any further, I stood at that kitchen counter, looked up, and said in my heart, "*If* this is the house for us, Lord, (by then I had the gut feeling that it was,) then I give it to You! You will have to take my fear of water away." Now I know that fear is not from God. He does not want us to have a spirit of fear, but of love and a sound mind. Therefore, I said, "I give this area of my fear to You. I surrender it, Lord. I also give my children to You." For the first time, I released my children into the Lord's hands and gave them back to God, realizing they are His children, and we are just babysitting them. Yes, I have a mother's heart, and I love them as all mothers love their children. I am concerned for them, but I do not carry fear for them because their lives are truly in God's hands. What freedom I felt.

Then I continued, "Lord, could you please take away this motion sickness because I sure don't want to be sick every day. I have a family to care for, college to attend, and work to do. If I am sick all of the time from watching that lake slosh around, I will not be able to function." This is a serious matter. Those of you who can relate, you know what a sick, gross feeling this is. For those of you who do not get motion sickness or never have and believe it is all in someone's head, you're right. It begins in your head, goes to your stomach, and then takes over your whole being. Honestly, I never wish anything bad on anyone; but if you'd had it just *once*, you would know what I mean and never doubt again.

As I continued with my pleas, I said, "Yes, Lord, take away my fear of water. Take away my motion sickness, and while You're at it, Lord, *please* teach me how to like *green*!" Yes! He did all three! He answered all of my requests.

On that day, I learned three lessons: submission, surrender, and serenity. Submission to the Lord and to my husband's wishes and decisions; and surrender of my will, my fears, and my children. Then I experienced the peace and serenity that it brings! Praise God!

I also learned very quickly that this was the perfect house for us. It was compact and efficient, with little or no up-keep inside or out. Who needed a big house to take care of? We were both going back to school. Bill was traveling back and forth to Chicago with his business. Our three kids were active in school and involved in sports. We were busy people. The Lord knew what we needed, so I gave that area of my life to the Lord in total submission, which shocked and pleased my husband very much. I was free from the fear of my children's future. The kids loved the lake. They swam, water skied, and enjoyed all of the water sports. I actually enjoyed the beauty of it too and wrote a poem about it, which I will share later on. I never did get in the water, though. Winona Lake is so dirty. It is the only lake where "anybody can walk on water."

I did not get motion sickness, and I honestly learned to love green. I found out that it means "praise and worship." I had my colors analyzed, and it is the most flattering color I can wear. I used green in every room of my house. Oh, what joy we can have when we *fully* trust Him and fully turn everything over to Him.

When I went back to our home in Mt. Prospect, I knew I had to have a surrender service now with my big blue house and all of my furniture. One Sunday, I was sitting in my beautiful living room. When the sun, through those soft, fluffy sheer "poufs" touched the chandelier, the crystals glistened and cast a spectrum of colors on my blue velvet sofa and chairs—how beautiful! Oh my, I felt like I was in heaven, my heavenly mansion. As I sat alone, I was reading Jill Briscoe's book, *There's a Snake in My Garden*. The Lord knew just what I needed. As I read her story about moving from England to the United States, I could relate because the contrast was that great for us too. I learned a great lesson on priorities and confirmed Matthew 6:33: "Seek ye first the Kingdom of God and His righteousness and *all* these things will be added to you" (emphasis added).

I thought of our lives, all we had been through, and how our heart's desire was to serve Him. Now God was opening the door. He was making a way for us. We were going to study so we could minister together.

What matters most in life? What really is most important? What stands in the way of complete surrender and total freedom? What area do we hang on to with our little finger, so afraid to let go? Is it our home, car, furniture, possessions, children, husband? Maybe even the past: hurts, anger, bitterness. The Lord wants us to lay at His feet these things. Hebrews 12:1–2 reads, "Lay aside the weights that are holding us back, anything that slows us down—especially those sins that wrap themselves so tightly around our feet and trip us up and let us run with patience the particular race that God has set before us." Here is the most important message in verse 2. "Keep your eyes on Jesus, our Leader and Instructor, the Author and Finisher of our faith." Oh my. Those verses have such a message for us. We need to examine ourselves as we make choices in life whether it is our everyday walk, or as Bill and I were taking a step of faith in this new life and ministry.

As I looked around at this room and this home in Mt. Prospect, I broke out in a tearful praise for the privilege of serving the Lord here. This was not only a house, but a home. We opened our home for a Ladies Bible study where ten to twelve women met every week. It was our blessing to have Delores Giannini as our leader. She had a sweet gentle spirit and a powerful presentation of God's Word. Most of us are still friends to this day. We also opened our home for the first back yard vacation Bible school. We were expecting twenty to thirty kids, and our yard was definitely large enough to handle that amount. Interesting that God would have it rain the first few days, so we welcomed the children inside. Much to our amazement, each day, the number increased to forty, fifty, sixty, and then seventy children! Every room was used. They even sat in circles on my white carpet in the living room. The garage and the basement were used for crafts. We even had to go down the street to our neighbors, and use their homes and garages when we split up into age groups. We had a fabulous team from our church who taught the lessons, crafts, games, and supplied the refreshments. We were so thankful for each one especially Gwen McNamara and Sandy McCall who planned, coordinated, opened and closed the program each day.

By Friday, when we invited the parents for the final program, there were more than one hundred and fifty people in our home. Thank You, Lord, for this opportunity. Many decisions to receive Christ were made that week, and we continued opening our home each year. The numbers increased as the children brought their friends. All we had to do was open our hearts and home and we did! We learned that when God blesses you with "things," they can be used for His glory. Our home was His! I thanked God for all of the people, especially the children, who heard the Gospel proclaimed. This house had been used by God through us to bring so many people closer to Him. Many, many people made decisions in this very room. To God be the glory for all He has done!

As I sat basking in that joy and peace, I released this home and all of "my" furniture to the Lord. I *totally* took my hands off the house. A wave of peace filled my heart as God brought into focus His plan for our lives. I opened my Bible to Isaiah 55 and read again the verses: "This plan of Mine is not what you would work out, neither are My thoughts the same as yours." Verse 9 says, "My ways are higher than yours and so are My thoughts higher than your thoughts. For just as the heavens are higher than the earth, so are My ways higher than yours." Verse 11 states: "My Word that I send out always produces fruit. It shall accomplish all I want to prosper everywhere I send it,"

The next verse, I hung on to and claimed for our move. Verse 12 reads, "So *you* will go out with joy. You will be led out in peace" (emphasis added). With that, I had complete victory and peace. I was able to let go and let God lead us. I sold most of my furniture and took only what I needed to our green cedar square home on Winona Lake. We left the big city, big house, our first church family and went forth with joy and peace.

Bill and I attended Grace College part time, two or three days a week on alternate days. Bill commuted between Winona Lake and Chicago to run his business. Finally, after two years, he brought the business to Winona Lake, and we began speaking on weekends at retreats and churches in the area. God kept the business going, which kept us self-supporting as we ministered in these small Midwest churches. Our children attended a Christian school and really, these were some of the best years of our lives.

I learned to love Winona Lake and spent many quiet moments having my devotions as I looked out at the awesome beauty of it. One particular day, the lake was so still it was like looking out at a mirror. You could see the reflection of trees, homes, and boats clear across to the other side. I thought, *How perfect and calm.* Then a thought came to me. *Isn't this just like our lives? When everything is peaceful and calm in our lives, people can see a clear reflection of Jesus in us. When things are going well, it is easy to see Him in us.*

Then all of a sudden, a huge cloud covered the clear blue sky, and it suddenly got dark. I thought, *Isn't this what happens in our lives?* Instantly, a dark cloud can come over us in the form of depression, bad or sad news, a crisis, or hurt and heartaches. Then the wind started to blow, causing the reflection to turn to large ripples. A storm was coming! And again, this is what sometimes happens in our lives when unexpected storms come. The reflection of Jesus turns into ripples of fear, doubt, anxiety, instability, and insecurity. Our reflection gets dim as the storm clouds come in. Sometimes these storms last for only a short time. Some are stronger, leaving more damage than others. This particular storm continued with loud claps of thunder, and the rain came down in torrents. Oh my. No sun, no reflection, no calmness—only turmoil. I thought, *What do we do at a time like this, Lord? Do we look to You, or do we look to the storm in our lives?*

As I pondered that thought, God gave me a powerful message from His Word. As quickly as the storm began that day, it passed. And behind that cloud, I saw a silver lining. In the clouds, I saw this beautiful rainbow across the lake. I sat there with tears in my eyes at the awesomeness of God and thought of His promise in Genesis 9:13–14, "I have placed My rainbow in the clouds as a sign of My promise. When I send clouds over the earth, the rainbow will be seen in the clouds and I will remember My promise to you." Yes, we will have storms in our life with dark days, distant thunder ripples that turn into waves of despair, but look at what He says. Our pot of gold at the end of the rainbow is His promises. Just as He promised in Genesis not to destroy the earth again with water, He promises to give us the Living Water found in His Word. After I saw the rainbow, I wrote the following:

> Lord, speak to me on this rainy day,
> Let me hear what You have to say.
> "Although the day is dark and the sun is not shining,
> I can assure you, there *will* be a silver lining.
> Don't expect peace from the world outside,
> For you'll only find it in My Word as you abide.

HOPE FOR THE DAYS AHEAD

The storms will come and the rain will fall,
But My message is the same for all.
I am the Way, the Truth and the Life,
Come unto *Me* and you will end all strife.

Those who are heavy laden and need a rest,
Trust in Me… I know what's best.
I will come and calm the stormy sea,
Just have the faith to believe in Me.

So look beyond this gloomy day,
And listen to what I have to say.
Through these lessons, you will learn,
A closer walk is what you will yearn.

How can you know the way of the cross,
Until you yourself have experienced some loss?
A loved one that you hold so dear,
Or perhaps your burden is finances this year.

Maybe there are problems between husband
 and wife,
Or you seem to have no meaning in life.
Have one of your children gone astray?
Look to Jesus this very day.

Whatever it is, the cross you will bear,
You need to remember, I *will* be there.
I will give you comfort and fill you with My
 love,
You will be lifted like the wings of a dove.

HANG ON! WE'RE HEADED FOR HAPPINESS!

You need to trust in Me, beyond your reach,
As I prepare you for the lessons you will teach.
There are so many people who need to know,
That I, Jesus Christ, love them so.

So as you walk along this pathway of life,
And go through some turmoil and strife,
Know it's for good and God's eternal glory,
Then you can go on and tell your victorious story."

Then we can thank the Lord for our circumstances!

Thank You, Lord

Now it doesn't matter if the sun isn't shining,
In my heart, there *is* a silver lining.
It doesn't matter if I have a cross to bear,
Jesus said He would be there.
His love and His light will always shine through,
With the Lord as my Guide, I know what to do.
I'll reach out and share His love with someone today.
And with confidence, I will say,
I have the answer to all your problems and fears,
It's found in *Jesus, He really cares.*
You won't have to search around anymore,
He'll give you what you're looking for.
Peace, joy, fulfillment, and comfort too.
It's up to you now—*what will you do?*

Will you turn to Jesus and have life evermore?
Or will you turn away and close the door?
Why don't you open your heart and let Him come in,
And then your life will truly begin.
May you receive the gift you have been longing for,
Jesus's love forevermore.

We spent ten wonderful years in Winona Lake. Along with raising three teenagers and attending Grace College, we were blessed to be "Mom and Pop" to many of the Grace students who were away from their families. Our home was always open to them for meals, talks, hugs, family fun, boat rides, and a place to hang out on weekends. To this day, we still cherish their friendships and relationships, along with their now grown families. We were also involved in a great evangelical church. Bill and the pastor would speak on Mondays at a luncheon open to the community. We, along with several other couples, brought in special speakers as an outreach for the area. I was involved in a ladies' prayer group and Bible study, which still meets to this day. What a precious, powerful, and prayerful group of ladies! Together, we led a Bible study for couples in our home. It was an awesome, exciting time! We felt like we were in the center of God's will and submissive to His leading. We heard a saying once which we have claimed: "God will never lead you where His grace cannot keep you." This was so true for us. He led us and kept us. To Him be the glory!

Chapter 5

A Great Discovery: We Can Be Different and Not Be Wrong

What I am about to share with you was one of the greatest discoveries of our lives, after the Lord, of course. It absolutely revolutionized our relationship with each other, our children, our family, and our friends. I *hope* it will do the same for you.

By 1975, Bill and I had come a long way in our marriage relationship. We were having devotions together; praying as a family; attending college; and taking Bible, marriage, and family classes. We were speaking at seminars and leading family retreats. Yes, we were moving right along in our Christian life. As always, God knows what we need next and who we need to meet to make an impact on our lives. In March of that year, several couples from our church were going to a retreat in southern Indiana. Bill and I didn't even know who the speakers were, but we were all looking forward to a wonderful weekend. Little did we know what God had in store for us.

I never will forget the first night and first hour. The speakers were introduced as Fred and Florence Littauer. What a sharp, dynamic, attractive couple they were. As Florence began talking (faster than most of us can think), I remember sitting on the edge of my seat, catching every word, and praising the Lord for this upbeat, powerful presentation. What an incredible story they had. We laughed, cried, and related so well.

After they finished sharing their lives with us, Florence asked a question that echoed in our ears, made us squirm, and kept us attentive for the rest of the evening. She said, "How many of you here have someone in your life that you would like to shape up, if you could?" We all looked around and should have stood up and said yes! But the murmur was loud enough to know that we all felt that way at one time or another or *always*, whatever the case may be. She continued on confirming that *all* of us do, but can we? The answer is no. As hard as we try and as much as we would like to, we just cannot change another person! A fact we all know down deep but just cannot seem to let go of.

Florence went on to describe the typical relationship and how most couples are opposites. It is a known fact that opposites attract, and soon after they are married, they begin to attack! We definitely are drawn together and are attracted to each other because of the strengths and good qualities in the other person. Subconsciously, we feel these strengths in our mate will compensate for our weak areas.

How does this work in a marriage? Not very well. In fact, in some cases, not at all. Remember I shared with you that Bill and I discovered on our honeymoon that we were the exact opposite and really had nothing in common, and that's why we had so many conflicts. We both wanted to be right! You see, this can be a serious problem especially when you are both strong in some areas and have definite ideas and opinions, and are not shy about expressing them. Bill thought I was wrong, and I thought he was wrong.

At that point, Florence made a statement that changed our focus and our lives. It is one that we have repeated hundreds

A GREAT DISCOVERY: WE CAN BE DIFFERENT AND NOT BE WRONG

of times as we share what Florence made so clear that night: "Do you realize that just because someone is different from you doesn't make them wrong?" She then went on to introduce us to the four basic temperaments: choleric, sanguine, melancholy, and phlegmatic.

Right now, I will *briefly* introduce you to the temperaments as explained in Florence Littauer's book, *Personality Plus*, which I recommend you read for a more in-depth study:

1. *Choleric.* The choleric person is an extrovert, a doer and an optimist. Cholerics are confident, self-sufficient, decisive, dominant, opinionated, strong-willed people, and can be sarcastic and impatient. They are very active, energetic, and productive. They have a take-charge, commanding personality; their goal in life is to have *control.* Their *obvious* needs in life are control and productivity. Their underlying need is to receive appreciation for their efforts. They are powerful workers, and their direction in life is to have *everything* their way, which they feel is the *right* way. They never think they are wrong, so they never say they are sorry. Their weakness is they control by anger. Their strength is that they are powerful workers. They are usually presidents of organizations or CEOs of companies, strong leaders, teachers, or are competitive in sports.
2. *Sanguine.* The sanguine person is a super-extrovert, a compulsive talker, and an eternal optimist. They exude enthusiasm and excitement. They have a magnetic personality. They do tend to exaggerate and embellish stories, and seem to be somewhat scatter-brained and disorganized. Their main goal in life is to *have fun!* They can actually turn disas-

ter into fun. Their direction in life is to have everything the happy way! Their obvious needs are to have excitement and fun. Their underlying needs are for approval and acceptance. Their weakness is that they control by *charm*. Their strength is that they are a popular talker. You will find sanguine most comfortable as hostesses, receptionists, or in sales. A sanguine is a "people person."

3. *Melancholy*. The melancholy is an introvert, a deep-thinker, and a pessimist. They are usually very sensitive, self-sacrificing, gifted, artistic, and creative. They have an analytical personality and can be moody, critical, and doubtful. Their main goal is to have *perfection*. Their direction in life is to have everything the perfect way. Their greatest obvious need is perfectionism and sensitivity. Their underlying need is to express themselves with a creative tenderness. Their weakness is that they manipulate by *moods*. Their strength is that they are a perfect thinker. Melancholy people make good CPAs, artists, musicians, and bankers.

4. *Phlegmatic*. The phlegmatic is also an introvert, a watcher, and a pessimist. They are calm, easy-going, laid back, passive, unmotivated, practical, dependable, friendly, but sometimes indecisive. They have a pleasing personality. Their goal in life is to achieve peace at any cost. They never rock the boat or make waves. Their direction in life is to take the *easy way*. Their obvious needs are to have peace and quiet. Their underlying need is for a sense of value as a person. Their weakness is to control by *procrastination*. Their strength is that they are peaceful mediators. You find the peaceful phlegmatic very content in the back-

A GREAT DISCOVERY: WE CAN BE DIFFERENT AND NOT BE WRONG

ground working in data entry, as a computer consultant, counselor, assembly line, or a program operator.

If we were to make a movie:

The *choleric* would be the director, in charge and in control.

The *sanguine* would be the actor, actress, on stage and up front.

The *melancholy* would be the producer, planned and perfect.

The *phlegmatic* would be the audience, content to be watching.

Just as an example, picture this: the four temperaments hanging a picture. The melancholy would have everything organized ahead of time: hammer, nails, tape measure, and ladder if needed. He would analyze the situation and would very accurately measure from wall to wall, ceiling to floor. Yes, it would be perfectly centered with only one nail hole in the wall.

The sanguine would have a problem from the beginning because he would not be able to find anything, unlike the melancholy who has a place for everything and everything is always put back in its place. The sanguine would be frantically looking for something that resembles a hammer (I myself have used "tools" such as a battery or the back of a knife or even a shoe—whatever works and is handy at the moment). *Measuring tape? Oh well, we'll just eyeball it.* Invariably, six holes later, the picture would be in the center. The sanguine would think, *Who cares about the holes? No one can see them, and it does make for a funny story when guests come.*

The choleric now would be exasperated because the picture had not been hung yet. He would take charge and find the biggest nail he could find. He too would use whatever he could find strong enough to hammer it in with because his sanguine wife still cannot find the hammer. Would he measure? Oh, no.

He would just whack it in anywhere. He would not care if the picture was centered, just as long as it was up and the job was done!

Then there's the phlegmatic who would have been sitting on the couch the whole time, watching and thinking about maybe getting up to do that little chore his wife had asked him to do weeks ago. Yep, just maybe he'll do it tonight. He'd say, "Honey, do you know where the hammer and nails are? No? Oh, okay. Guess I'll have to do it some other time. Maybe next week. I'm going to take a nap now, okay?"

Can you see how frustrating this can be with just simple things like hanging a picture? Compound that with trillions of other little things, and you have *one* big, major problem called irreconcilable differences. That's why we feel a study and understanding of the temperaments is important in every marriage and relational circumstance.

Are you getting "the picture"? Well, we sure were as we began to see ourselves in a different light and way. It began to make sense that, yes, just because we were different, that didn't make us wrong. There are no wrong temperaments. What we found as most people do, was that we are a combination of two, having strengths and weaknesses in each one, with one being a little more dominant. Bill is choleric-sanguine, and I am sanguine-choleric. We could hardly wait to hear the rest of the seminar.

We were so excited about this newfound information and related so well to Fred and Florence, we decided to meet them during the break. Well, needless to say, it was instant rapport. With our outgoing personalities and newfound temperaments, we could tell this was going to be an instant friendship and, of course, pre-planned by God. Fred and Florence invited us to sit at their table for breakfast the next morning, and we began to share our dreams of having a ministry for couples and families.

A GREAT DISCOVERY: WE CAN BE DIFFERENT AND NOT BE WRONG

They were a great source or encouragement for us and were so helpful with ideas and resources. They really took us under their wings and that was the beginning of a long and lasting friendship.

Through the years, we invited them back to Indiana to speak at our church and share these principles. Each time was very special, but one occasion stands out as a highlight as it related so well to understanding the temperaments in a family situation, ours. By now, we had given the evaluation to just about everyone we knew, including our two older children, Bill and Bonnie, who were eighteen and twenty at the time. Our youngest, Jay, who was seventeen, had not yet taken it. It was no surprise to us that we four were a mixture of choleric and sanguine, some stronger in one than the other. So needless to say, our normal life and conversations were very powerful, very controlling, very talkative, and very loud, but always fun (well, most of the time). We all interrupted each other, and sometimes we would have four stories going at the same time. Confusing to some, but we understood and we always came back and finished each one. To this day, my daughter and I can run on five tracks, always coming back to the "main station." The sanguines in our family tried to make everything fun, but the choleric in charge did not always see it that way. So here is the scene: four outgoing, talkative, power-plus people having fun and then there's Jay, our youngest, who is very quiet and shy sometimes. He did not say much up to this point. In fact, he used to say that life in our house was like being at a Baskin-Robbins ice cream store, where you had to take a number to have a turn to talk! We did not know he wanted to talk, we just thought he was the quiet one. Little did we know at that time that we intimidated him so much that he just very quietly sat back and watched us do our thing.

On this particular occasion when Fred and Florence were staying with us, I remember Florence observing our "normal" family situation and saw us in our powerful performances. She then turned to Jay and said, "Jay, I'm very interested to know what temperament you are. Could we sit down and go over the evaluation together?" He was a little overwhelmed but liked the special attention he was getting. We all looked in amazement as we didn't think he cared enough to be interested. We thought he *liked* being the quiet one. What a revelation for us all!

After about a half hour, we saw Jay jump up from the floor where they were sitting, waving his paper excitedly in his hand, shrieking, "I'm a sanguine! I'm a sanguine!" We looked wide-eyed in shock, really. Our quiet, shy, little Jay was a sanguine?

"Oh, yes," Florence said. "He is! And a cute one at that!" She looked at us and said, "All four of you are so powerful and outgoing, you unknowingly intimidated him. You didn't mean to, but it did happen." We stood there, realizing more than ever how important it was to know your temperament strengths and weaknesses, especially in a family.

Just think what a positive effect this will have with each child's self-worth, knowing that just because they are different doesn't make them wrong. This is so crucial when parents have such high expectations for their children and want them to be "just like me" when sometimes, they are the exact opposite and just can't be. Now the same is true when children are exactly like their parents. They can clash if they are both strong or never communicate if they are both passive. You see the danger in both of these. Also, as in our case, children sometimes do not express who they really are out of fear, intimidation, or just introverted habits and patterns. I strongly suggest that if you haven't already, read Florence's book *Raising the Curtain on Raising Children*. You will find it to be of great help to you. As

A GREAT DISCOVERY: WE CAN BE DIFFERENT AND NOT BE WRONG

parents, we look back and see how these truths affected all of our children in a positive way.

This discovery was life changing for Jay. It gave him such confidence to know he was like us, which he wanted to be to feel part of our family in an understanding and relational way. This gave him such self-confidence. His whole countenance changed. That was in March of his junior year of high school. In April, he went on a spring break trip to Florida with his class and had a great time. He was free to have fun and be himself. Everyone loved his newfound personality and that was the beginning of his confident, outgoing expression of life.

As I think back, Jay was creative and sensitive as a child—always doing just enough to get by and have fun without getting into *real* trouble. I think the word is "mischievous"! When we were called in for parent-teacher conferences, none of us could keep a straight face when we discussed Jay's jargons. I am so thankful his true temperament was rediscovered at just the right time, and to know we Buftons are all a combination of the same traits—sanguine and choleric.

Our daughter, Bonnie, was eighteen at the time and dating her future husband. It was so helpful in their relationship because she is choleric-sanguine, and he is melancholy-phlegmatic. Very opposite, but again, this is natural to be attracted to one another. The deep-thinking, easy-going individual is attracted to the outgoing, social butterfly who likes to have fun and take charge. The phlegmatic knows they will not have to be entertaining in a group of friends, and they will not have to make too many trivial decisions if they are hooked up with a sanguine spouse. On the other hand, the spirited sanguine needs the easy going, sensible stability of the melancholy-phlegmatic personality. Together, they can complement one another rather than compete with one another as Bill and I did.

In our case, we are both strong personalities: Bill, being choleric-sanguine, and I, being sanguine-choleric. This is very difficult in a relationship if you do not know the Lord, and you do not have an understanding of the basic temperaments. You can see now why we really believed we were right and the other, wrong. What a difference it made in our relationship when we learned how to complement one another instead of competing with each other. Each of us had different gifts and strengths. When we recognized what these were, we had the freedom to allow each other to use them freely. As a result, we were able to minister more effectively and live in a harmonious way. In fact, it became fun.

Like any good concept, the temperament theory is not a cure-all for everything. However, it is one of the best tools for helping individuals understand and accept others as they are, and to accept themselves. It gives you a better understanding of who you are and why you act the way you do. It is never to be used as an excuse of your behavior saying, "Oh, that's just the way I am. I'm sanguine (or choleric or melancholy or phlegmatic)." Do not let your weakness overwhelm you and make you feel there is no hope for you. Rather, use it to give you hope and help for self-improvement and self-acceptance.

Caution: this is for *you* only. It is not to be used to correct or change another person or even to categorize them for that matter. We need to develop our self-worth in Christ and receive His acceptance and then in turn, accept and "love others as ourselves." We need to develop a sincere interest and love for other people, seeing them and us as God sees us. "Man looks at the outward appearance, but God looks at our heart" (1 Sam. 16:7).

How I wish we knew about the personality traits when we got married. We would have avoided a lot of heartache and hurt. That is why Bill and I taught a class for engaged couples at

A GREAT DISCOVERY: WE CAN BE DIFFERENT AND NOT BE WRONG

our church called Fit to be Tied! How appropriate. In all of our years of teaching and counseling, we have yet to see two people who are planning to get married be of the same temperament. There may be, but we have not met one. Invariably, they are opposite. We are subconsciously drawn to the strengths of the other person because we know this will cover our weaknesses. This can be to our advantage if we use the strengths to compliment the relationship. Together, you can accomplish great things. The ideal is to accept each other's weaknesses and adjust to them. This is not easy, but it can be done. Remember with God, all things are possible.

That is why we teach these personality principles *first* in our premarital classes. It even helps in planning for the wedding. There, you normally have six or more people involved—both sets of parents and some well-meaning friends. Here again, you can see how this can be a problem, not only with different temperaments, but different ideas brought in from your backgrounds. We have known many cases where the families are not even speaking by the day of the wedding because of so many differences. This does not have to be. If we would have an understanding of the temperaments and not put such unrealistic expectations on people, we would all get along better in every area of our lives.

What is so great is when we realize we all need each other. Each one brings a special uniqueness to a relationship. God, in fact, created us for a special purpose with different gifts, talents, and temperaments. As Florence says in her book *Personality Plus*:

> God did not intend us all to be sanguine. We'd have lots of fun, but never be organized. God did not make us all choleric leaders. If He had, there would be no followers. God did

not want us all to be a perfect melancholy, for if things went wrong, we'd all be depressed. God did not want us all to be laid back like the phlegmatic, or nothing would get done.

God created us all different so that we would complement one another and complete the Body of Christ. Ephesians 4:15–16 says it so clearly, "Christ is the head of the body—the church. Under His direction the whole body is fitted together perfectly, and each part, in its own special way, helps the other parts so that the whole body is healthy and growing full of love." That is the way it should be in the home. When each member knows who he is in Christ and then looks at *their* own strengths and weaknesses—not everyone else's—then, and only then, can we function properly and have peace and harmony.

If you want change in your home, let it begin with *you*. The Bible says in Psalm 139, "Examine me, oh Lord. Point out anything in me that makes You sad." Then we need to begin to compliment one another's strengths instead of criticizing their weaknesses. Do not be in constant competition with one another but rather work toward being compatible by thinking of the other person's needs before your own, honoring and perfecting one another.

The Bible has a lot to say about our actions: Ephesians 5:15–17 states, "So be careful how you act—these are difficult days. Don't be fools. Be wise. Make the most of every opportunity you have for doing good. Don't act thoughtlessly, but try to find out and do whatever the Lord wants you to do." With His help and the Holy Spirit in us, we can complete the work that He has called us to do. For families, that is to have a Christ-centered home; and for singles, it is to have a Christ-centered life and live for Him. The key is to be Spirit-controlled, as some

A GREAT DISCOVERY: WE CAN BE DIFFERENT AND NOT BE WRONG

would say. Christ is our life, and the Holy Spirit in us gives us the power to live victoriously over self.

Think about each temperament with Christ in control. God uses the choleric in a mighty way as Christian leaders, teachers, pastors, speakers, and evangelists. When the choleric is yielded to the Lord, he is used in a powerful way for God's glory.

God uses the spirited sanguine to uplift and encourage people with their enthusiasm and excitement. They are never at a loss for something to say for the cause of Christ.

The meticulous melancholy is perfect for pre-planning and organizing all of the details in life. You can depend on them to analyze all of the obstacles before they proceed with a plan. They do follow through to the end.

Oh, and yes, God uses the peaceful phlegmatic to bring stability to the other temperaments. They do have a gentle, quiet spirit, and they do not look for credit, which is one of the greatest Christ-like qualities—humility.

Yes, God uses each one of us to carry out His purpose. These principles and temperaments are helpful whether single or married, young or old. Think about the workplace and how beneficial this would be when someone applies for a job. In fact, there are many companies and organizations who give this or a similar evaluation to their prospective employees. You want the person to work in a position where they feel gifted and comfortable.

For instance, you would not want a sanguine in charge of details, money or meticulous, mundane jobs. No, that is a job for the melancholy, who thrives on details and perfection. He likes accounting, banking, and filling in little columns and spaces in a quiet office.

The sanguine, on the other hand, is best when talking with people, so put her up front as a receptionist, greeting people, or being a tour guide, salesperson, speaker, or emcee—anything spontaneous and centered around people and activity.

The phlegmatic is good at a slow, steady pace. No deadlines or competition. Computers and data processing are very good careers for the phlegmatic. They make good counselors because they are such good listeners. Remember, they are spectators, not competitors like the choleric.

Give a choleric a challenge a day and they will love it. They are motivated to act on the spot. Never tell a choleric it cannot be done. They thrive on obstacles and impossible situations.

Do you see how important it is to know your strengths and weaknesses, gifts and talents? Can you understand also how this affects every area of your life, whether you are married or single, in the work place or at home? We can now look at others in a different way. For the first time, we can say, "Hey, that person isn't wrong. They are just different from me." As we think about our self-image, we can say, "I'm not wrong. I'm just different from you, and it's okay!"

I would strongly encourage you, if you haven't already, to read more about these fabulous findings. They will transform your temperaments and revitalize your relationships in a *positive, perfect, peaceful, powerful* way!

Chapter 6

Help! I'm a Parent!

I know of no greater calling that comes with both an awesome privilege and overwhelming responsibility than that of being a parent. Yes, God has chosen some of us to "babysit" His children. They truly are God's special gifts to us as it says in Psalm 127:3, "Children are a gift from God." For those of you who have these gifts, may I give you *Hope for the Days Ahead* in raising them; God does have a plan. In the proceeding pages, We will share with you His plan and principles, and how they worked in the lives of our children. May this chapter encourage parents that there is hope and that it is never too late!

Our search for help led us to the cross and to His Word which gives us instructions on how to train up a child. We also attended seminars and retreats on the family and took classes to learn how to be godly parents. The results were phenomenal as today, each of our children know Christ as their Savior, have Christian mates, and are raising their children according to God's Word.

Bill and I have summarized the following thoughts and principles that will turn your frustration into hope. With God's help and your commitment and consistency, you can begin to build a strong foundation of love, acceptance, and worth with your children. The lines of communication will stay open through the years. Remember, it is never too late to begin.

God's plan and principles for parents

1. *Parents need to be a consistent example.* Kids do not buy the saying "do as I say, not as I do" routine, and they do not respect the parent who does this. We teach what we are. The truths of our faith must be seen, lived, and taught in the home. What our kids see happening in the home is how they pattern their lives. The biggest thing parents want from their children is respect, but respect is earned. The parent must be an example and follow the guidelines that God sets up for us. "Live the life and walk the talk." This can come only through Christ's example in us. Even when you do blow it, and we all do, your children will respect you for "admitting it and continue on practicing what you preach." They need you to be consistent and fair in your relationships.

    Our eldest son, Bill, told us, "I want to teach my sons like you taught me. You have been an example to me of consistency and fairness. I want to follow the same guidelines by which you taught us."

2. *Parents need to build healthy relationships with their children.* This has to start with LAW—*l*ove, *a*cceptance, and *w*orth. When these foundations are established in the home, they will not have to look for them in other people like their peers, school, jobs, or achievements. They also will not look for them in drugs, alcohol, or sex. If we as parents establish this LAW at a young age, they will respond to it and will always come back to it

as it says in Proverbs 22:6, "Train up a child in the way they should go and when they are old, they will not depart from it."

a. Love them

Begin by telling them daily, "I love you." Say it by compliments—"You did a great job." "You look beautiful." "You're so handsome." Say it by outward affection—hug them, put your arm around them (they're never too old). We do this with our children to this day and have begun with our grandchildren. Begin when they are little: lift them up, cuddle them, hold them, put them on your lap, and give them loving hugs. This builds security, acceptance, and a sense of belonging.

b. Acceptance

Accept them for who they are, not for what they do. Let your loving acceptance be as Jesus's for us—unconditional. Not, "I'll love you *if* you do this, *if* you say this, *if* you act this way, *if* you look right, dress right, act right." This is performance-based acceptance. Now we are not to condone or overlook rebellious actions or sinful choices. These need to be addressed and dealt with. They need to know that God says those whom He loves, He disciplines. This is where tough love comes in. If you establish the love and security they need at a young age, they will not stray too far from it.

c. Worth

They need to know who they are in Christ first, and then in the family unit. Let them know they are worth something to God and to you. They are important, they have a place, and they individually complete your family. Let them know that you care for them and will be there for them. Our youngest child, Jay, said, "You were always there for me, loving me and accepting me whether I was right or wrong. You were there to help me not to make the same mistakes over and over. I pray that I can be that kind of example to my children too."

3. *Parents must be consistent in loving discipline.* Discipline should be related to love and acceptance as our Heavenly Father loves, accepts, and disciplines us. Proverbs 3:12 states, "For who the Lord loves, He disciplines." Discipline should provide structure, guidance, protection, consistency, and fairness. Set guidelines first, and then follow through with the discipline. Punishment should be fair and in line with the act of disobedience. Follow through at the time of disobedience. We did not "spare the rod and spoil the child"; but it was done in a controlled, firm, and loving manner, letting them know it was for their ultimate good. We always hugged and prayed afterward. This was tough, but it worked!

4. *Parents need to communicate with their children.* Communication is two-fold—listening and talking. Too often, as we counsel teens, we hear, "My parents won't listen to me." Listening is the first step to communication.

Listening in love:

a. *Take* time or *make* time to listen to them.
b. Uninterrupted time alone with them is meaningful and very productive, giving them your complete attention.
c. Respect their opinion and privacy.
d. Encourage them to share honestly and openly.
e. Do not make fun of their ideas. Do not pre-judge or have pre-conceived thoughts.
f. Listen with an understanding spirit.
g. Come to an agreeable solution.

Talking:

a. Set aside quality time after you have established trust and a caring attitude.
b. Let them share and express their feelings, good and bad, excitements, and disappointments. This assures them that you value their ideas.

Our daughter, Bonnie said, "Mom and Dad had a vital interest in our lives especially during our prayer times. These were times of sharing, caring, and wanting to know what was happening in our individual worlds. We talked about everything, from work to school to dates. We could share openly, even complaints and frustrations. Then we would all pray for one another. I also appreciated my special date nights with my dad. We would go to a fancy restaurant or just out for pizza. I always felt like I was special and important."

This brings us to the last, but most important principle and definitely God's plan for us.

5. *Parents need to pray with and for their children.* Care enough to pray for each other. This is a vital and important aspect in the circle of the family. You have heard the old saying, "The family that prays together, stays together." We really believe that is true. This is the greatest gift you can give each other, to know you care enough to pray for one another. Start when they are young.

   a. Set aside a time when you, as a family, can pray together.
      I know this gets difficult as they get older and have so many places to go and commitments, but if this is established at a young age, it will be the foundation they need. Even if all of the family members cannot be there, do it anyway.

   b. Keep it simple, and not too long.
      We always had a time when each one could share openly about what was going on in their lives. It could be a time of sharing, a short devotional, conversational prayer, reading scripture, or maybe having just one person pray. This was our time of open communication with the family, allowing them to express their feelings, fears, and praying for God's will for their futures.

   c. Pray for others.
      We always prayed for other family members, the kid's friends and of course, for each other. This builds a strong bond between them and as a family.

Bill and I believe that prayer is the foundation for family living and that foundation is to be based on the truths of God's Word and in a personal relationship with Jesus Christ. The Christian home is not only where Christians live, but where Christ lives. Christ living in us is the basis we need to live this life. "Not I, but Christ in us." That's why we firmly believe we need to impart these truths to our children preferably at a young age, or as soon as possible. God honors our commitment to do this and has a plan for you to follow. We are here to say—it works! You can have contentment with your children and fun instead of frustration!

Content with your children

The Bible is clear that children are truly God's special gifts to us as it says in Psalm 127:3, "Children are a gift from God—they are His reward." He did reward us with three fantastic children—not perfect by any means, as we are not perfect either. But as I look back and think of all the things that could have happened to them as a result of our behavior and lifestyle for ten years, I humbly praise Him for how they turned out.

Each one of our children is unique and very special, just as yours are. They are all different with different personalities, temperaments, talents, abilities, likes, and dislikes. We love each one of them the same amount, but in different ways. Each is a *special* gift from God and each one we cherish in that way. This book would not be complete unless I shared briefly about each one of their lives, not to boast or brag, but to give glory to God!

Bill was our firstborn—the firstborn is always special! We were thrilled that he was a boy, and we named him after his father. He was born three days before his dad's birthday, and Bill was so proud to have a son. He was really a good kid—easy to train and minded pretty well. Normal challenges, yes, but he always respected our discipline.

Growing up, Bill loved sports and played basketball, baseball, football, and soccer. His dad was thrilled, of course, and went to all of his games. That love for sports continued and is now his profession. He has dedicated his life to teaching, coaching, and mentoring young people.

I remember the time Bill and I received a letter from him saying, "Molding young men and women—what a responsibility. I know it is what God wants me to do. What a ministry I have with the kids here. Thanks for the example and standards you set for me. I love you both and appreciate all you have done in molding me into what I am today. What great teachers and coaches I had in you, Mom and Dad. I just wanted to say thanks for all the help, spiritually, financially, and mentally, during the all the years. I could have never made it without you. I've grown up so much from the time I left home at the age of eighteen. I went to three schools, had many coaches, found a great wife, and learned much about responsibility. I'm glad I had a great home and relationship with my parents."

Bill and his wife, Sally, live in Colorado and are the parents of five children: Beau, Brett, Alexandra, Ashlyn, and Alyson. We thank God for each one of them and how they are raising their children in the ways of the Lord! As a result, they all have asked Jesus into their hearts.

Bonnie is our second child and only girl, and she is special too. She was born in 1962, on April Fool's Day. What fun that was! No one would believe us when we told them we had a beautiful baby girl with black hair and big brown eyes. We named her Bonnie Jean, and she became the apple of her dad's eye and the joy of my heart. She was a sweet and darling baby, and always turned heads with her sparkling eyes and adorable smile. She was easy to discipline, had a teachable spirit, and was always ready to help me with everything. That continued as she grew, we worked together, spoke together for Mother-Daughter banquets and become "good friends."

I remember in her senior year of high school, she was wondering what her future held and what the years ahead would bring—college, career, or marriage. As we all do, she began to make plans, asking God to bless them. One was for college, one was for a career, and one was for a "date before the end of the year." One evening, she was sharing these with me. I said, "Bonnie, do not stand in the way of God bringing a *blessing* into your life. You need to let go of all of these plans and say, 'Lord, You direct me, You lead me, You have the best plan for me.'" We prayed that night, and she did let go of all these areas.

It was about three weeks later when she came home from a basketball game and said, "Oh Mom, you won't believe it, but I met the most gorgeous guy. He has blond hair, big blue eyes, and he even drives a black Trans Am (seems these things are important and make a big impression at that age)."

I said, "That sounds great, Bonnie, and what is his name?"

She said, "Mom, you'll never believe it. His name is Dave *Blessing!*"

I thought, *Oh Lord, You do have a sense of humor,* as I remembered my statement a few weeks back: "Don't let your will stand in the way of God bringing a blessing into your life." She surrendered, and He did just that!

Dave and Bonnie were married in 1981. They have three children: David William, Jonathan Jay, and Jennifer Joy. Yes, we do "count our blessings and name them one by one," and see what God has done. David and Bonnie live in Indiana, and they too have established a Christian home with good family values. All three children have accepted Jesus into their hearts.

Jay, our youngest son, was born nineteen months after Bonnie. I remember Bill's Dad saying, "That boy will bring you more joy in life," and that, he has. Jay is one of those special kids that every family should have—creative and sensitive. What mischief he hasn't done hasn't been invented yet! Discipline was not a word in his vocabulary—never doing bad things, just mischievous and spontaneous. He loved sports too and was quite a natural athlete.

His desire also was to be a teacher and a coach. He wrote this in a recent letter to his dad: "You taught and encouraged me in all the sports I've played and have been there to cheer and support me too. You have shown me how to be a good husband and friend to my wife by your and Mom's example throughout the years. I just pray that I can be as good a husband, father, and example to my wife and children as you have been to me."

Jay and his wife Denise are the proud parents of three children: Rebecca Marie, Dana Lyn, and BJ, named after Bill and Great-Grandpa John. Thankfully, they also have come to know the Lord as their Savior, and they have asked Jesus into their hearts.

We began praying for Christian mates for *all* of our children very early in their lives, and I know God answered in giving us Sally, Dave, and Denise. We love them all very much and are so thankful to have them as part of our family. God's choice—our blessing! How thankful I am when I look back and see God's faithfulness in the lives of our children. We do praise Him for how they have turned out. Their examples should give hope to parents everywhere because Bill and I were far from perfect parents, but God's Grace abounds and with Him all things are possible.

In 1967, when our marriage was falling apart and we were about ready to go our separate ways, these three children kept us together and made us realize that we needed help. We did not have a secure foundation for them. Our lives were falling apart because of our selfish behavior, and it was definitely affecting our children.

I have to honestly say that it was these precious faces that made us realize that we needed help. I saw how our selfishness was affecting their lives, and I began my spiritual search. As I said in the previous chapter, it ended at the cross, when I found Jesus Christ. My search ended when my new life began. We tell parents everywhere that it's never too late—start now! With God's help, you can turn your frustration into a firm foundation in the Lord.

Chapter 7

From Fiscal Failure to Financial Freedom: That Makes Good Cents

I'm sure all of you can relate to a time in your life when all is going well. You are on top of the world, so to speak. Your marriage relationship is going great, kids are doing fine, business is at its peak. You are healthy, wealthy, and wise, as they say. Things seem too good to be true. Uh-oh. Watch out. Hang on! It may be the calm before the storm. The storms did come for us—in fact, it was more like an earthquake.

During the mid- to late-1980s, the economy became shaky, and small businesses began to suffer. We could no longer compete with the big companies. Bill could see it coming, and we began to pray. In fact, many days, especially on Thursdays, I remember praying for money to come in to meet our payroll; and *every time*, God would miraculously meet our needs.

We once had a man come in during the week and ask us if we wanted to sell our rooming house, a piece of income property we had bought earlier that year. Bill pondered a moment and remembered he had it for sale once before, but no one offered to buy it. Now, when we needed the money, God sent

FROM FISCAL FAILURE TO FINANCIAL FREEDOM: THAT MAKES GOOD CENTS

a buyer. They agreed on a price, and he gave us a check to hold it. Yes, that down payment was just enough to cover our payroll for the week. God is never too soon or too late but always on time, just as He promises.

I well remember, months later, when we were trying to sell our business and we thought many times *we* had the perfect buyers. At the last minute, it would fall through. This went on for nine long months from January to August, and each time, *we* expected it to be sold. It was another test of our faith to meet our payments every month. At just the right time, we would sell a piece of machinery that would cover our overhead for that month.

By the morning of August 1 of 1983, we had exhausted *all* of *our* resources and equipment. I was having my quiet time on my knees. Actually, it wasn't too quiet as I was desperately crying out to God saying, "Lord, Lord, I know You know our situation. I know 'all things *are* working together for good,' *but Lord,* this is it! We can't go any further. We are at the end of ourselves."

I chuckle now because isn't that just where God wants us—at the end of ourselves? Oh, often we think we are there; we think we have surrendered all. But as we look back and search our hearts, many times, there are areas we are still hanging on to.

So on this day in early August, I asked the Lord to show me something in His Word for that day. Now I know what you are thinking: does He *really* do that? Well, I have to say, He does and will for anyone. "Seek and you shall find." I did search the scriptures and read in Haggai 2:18–19: "But note this: from today this twenty-fourth day of the ninth month; from this day I will bless you. I am giving you this promise now even before you have begun to re-build the temple structure [which we felt was our lives and business]." Now I know what Haggai and his people did, but I'm telling you what I did. I obeyed! I claimed that for us and our business.

That very week, Bill got a call from a large company nearby, saying they were interested in purchasing our business and building. In my devotions for that morning, I read Psalm 20:4–5: "May He grant you your heart's desire and fulfill all your plans. May there be shouts of joy when we hear the news of your victory, flags flying with praise to God for all He has done for you. May He answer all your prayers!" And He did! My prayers were Psalm 62: "I stand silently before the Lord waiting for Him to rescue us. Why should I be tense when trouble comes?" Verse 7: "My protection and success comes from God alone. He is my refuge. Oh, my people trust Him all the time. Pour out your longings before Him, for He can help!" And He did! Yes, the business deal went through; and believe it or not, we signed the final papers on *August 24*, the very day the Lord said He would bless us. He was true to His word as always! We gave Him all the praise and glory. He answered our prayers as He said He would in Psalm 20, and His promises for us are also for you.

I know many of you may be desperate and struggling financially right now. Maybe you have lost your job and do not even know where the next check will come from. Maybe you are close to losing your business or your home. I do understand. May I encourage you and give you *Hope for the Days Ahead*? Our God is a faithful God. He *will* meet your needs. I do not know exactly how, but I know He will. May I suggest you seek Christian financial counsel at your church or a church in your area? They can give you advice and help during this time of need. Search the financial section at your Christian bookstore for books relating to biblical principles on finances. There are also many support groups available. You do not need to go through this alone. Consider seeking advice from those who can help you get on your feet again.

Some of you may be in a situation where you have to sell your home. This may be God saying, "Trust Me with even that." We found ourselves in a similar situation. We began to feel a need to lay aside the things that were holding us back from financial freedom, and our big home on the lake was one of them. So that summer, we put it on the market to sell. *We thought the timing was best with all of the summer crowd there and the activities going on. Who wouldn't be enticed by this home on beautiful Winona Lake?

Well, it did not sell by September, October, or November. I remember well. On a cold November evening, Bill said, "Jeannie, we just have to sell this house by December 27. We cannot go any farther. We do not need this big house anymore. We need to be free from these house payments." Our children were grown, and it was just the two of us in a 3,500 square foot home.

Yes, it was the right thing to do. I thought, *Nothing is too hard for You, Lord! You have delivered us before—You can do it again! Show me in Your Word what You are going to do.* Oh, the powerful Word of God! Run to it, read it, meditate on it, claim it, live it, share it. That is what I am doing now—sharing with you how powerful it is and how God's promises are true for us today.

In November of 1983, as I was reading in my Bible (in fact, I have the date marked in red), I turned to Habakkuk. Whoever reads Habakkuk? I had not, until that day. I found a powerful message in Habakkuk 1:5, "The Lord replied, 'Look and be amazed! You will be astounded at what I am about to do! For I am going to do something in your lifetime that you will have to see to believe!'"

Oh, I like that! I thought, *What could it be, Lord?* I read on and found this message in chapter 2, verse 3: "But these things I plan won't happen right away. Slowly, steadily, surely, as the time approaches, when the vision will be fulfilled. If it seems *slow, do not despair,* for these things will surely come to pass. Just be patient! They won't be overdue one single day" (emphasis added)! Oh my! I was so excited I could hardly contain myself.

I immediately accepted and claimed that for us by faith. I didn't know how in the world God was going to do it, but I knew He would. I gave it to Him and trusted it with Him. I "let go and let God." Just wait until you hear how He did it! This is the greatest testimony of His faithfulness.

Every Christmas, we would go to Illinois, to my parents' home. It was December 24, Christmas Eve, a cold and snowy day. Bill had been sick for a few days and had gone to the doctor that morning to get some medicine so he could travel. When he came home, he told me that the doctor said he couldn't go anywhere. He had a high fever and a contagious virus. So he stayed in Indiana, and the kids and I traveled to Illinois. Does God use sickness and high fevers to complete His plan? You bet He does! He works through *all* things!

I remember the day we were driving to Illinois. My son-in-law, Dave, asked if Bill and I were still thinking about moving to California. We had been thinking about it. In fact, we had always wanted to live there and were seriously considering it. I told Dave that we were waiting on the Lord to open the door and sell our house. I was thinking to myself, *You have only two days left, Lord!* I wondered who was going to buy our house or any house over Christmas, in the dead of winter. Remembering His promise, I tried to put it out of my mind, *rest* in Him, and enjoy the next few days.

FROM FISCAL FAILURE TO FINANCIAL FREEDOM: THAT MAKES GOOD CENTS

On December 26, as we were getting ready to drive back home, Bill called. He said, "You're not going to believe this, but I got a call from a realtor and he wants an exclusive listing on our house for seventy-two hours. He thinks he has a potential buyer. In fact, they want to see the house tomorrow (the twenty-seventh of December)." This was too much! *Lord, You do have a sense of humor! Only You, Lord, could take this impossible situation, turn it around, and "make all things possible."* I got home that evening and got the house in order, re-read my verse, affirmed it, and claimed it again.

The next morning, the lady interested in our home came over at ten o'clock. She returned with her husband at noon, and by six o'clock that evening, we had an offer. By seven o'clock the evening of December 27, our house was sold! *Praise the name of Jesus!* In Him will I trust. *Remember,* "these things will surely come to pass. *Just be patient,* they won't be overdue, not *one single day!*" I truly believe He allowed us to experience this so that we could in turn help others and give hope and encouragement in their times of great need. "My God shall supply your needs" (Phil. 4:19).

Yes, God does promise to meet our needs, and He also tells us not to worry about tomorrow. However, He does want us to be wise, to sensibly plan for the future. We also need to be good stewards of the monetary gifts which He has given us. We are to understand that God owns everything. James 1:17 says, "Every good and perfect gift comes from God." This relates to financial things as well as spiritual things, just as He wants us to go into all the world and share the Gospel. He also wants us to share our earnings by giving back a portion to Him. The norm for a Christian is ten percent of their earnings, but we are also to be accountable for the other ninety.

I love the story of RG LeTourneau from Longview, Texas. He owned an earth-moving company and wrote a book called

Mover of Men and Mountains. In it, he shares his thoughts on the ten-percent principle. He said that if God can live on ten percent, so could he. So he gave ninety percent of his earnings to the Lord's work, and he lived on ten percent. He became a multimillionaire and started LeTourneau College in Texas. Now I know this is the extreme and is unusual, but I do know this: you cannot out-give God. Whatever you give in time, talent, or tithe, He returns it to you. Proverbs 11:24 states, "It is possible to give away and become richer! It is also possible to hang on too tightly and lose everything. Yes, the generous man will prosper. By refreshing others, he will refresh himself."

In our search for financial freedom, Bill was asked to give a seminar on finances. As he prepared for this timely message, these resources were revealed to us, and I hope they will be helpful to you:

1. *Resources.* There are many resources to help you and will give you good advice and guidelines such as books written by Christian authors and seminars given by financial advisers on how to manage your money. These will be *very* helpful to you, but the best resource is the Bible. The Word of God tells us much about money. Some people think that money is the root of all evil; that is not true. The Bible says the *love* of money is the root of all evil. When money becomes someone's god and takes first place in their lives before faith, family, and their future, this is when it becomes the "root of all evil." We must have our priorities in order and have the proper attitude about money. This principle is true when the tables are turned, and there is a lack of money. When all of our monetary resources have run out, it can cause a person to stop trusting and turn away from the Lord, thinking God has failed them. Again, we cannot lose sight of who the Giver of all things is and then remember our number one priority is to seek first the Kingdom

of God. When we get our focus back on Him and strip off anything that holds us back and trips us up from running the race God has set before us (as it says in Hebrews 12:1–2), then we can learn to revise our lives and set realistic goals with our priorities in order.

2. *Revise.* After we read all of our resource material, we then need to set realistic goals and revise our budget to make it compatible with our income. Be specific and consistent. You cannot live on the "feast or famine" routine. The roller coaster way of life causes instability and insincerity. Careless overspending causes many marital problems, especially if each one comes from different upbringings relating to money, which is the case in most marriages. One person is usually conservative and one is extravagant. That is why you should create a balanced, workable formula that can realistically be achieved by both the husband and wife. In fact, financial discipline should be taught to all family members starting at a young age. Then they can work together to achieve the goals that are set. Sometimes, we set our goals too high, and we get into trouble. The Bible tells us in Luke 14:28, "Don't begin until you count the cost, for who would begin construction of a building without getting estimates and then checking to see if he has enough money to pay the bills." Verse 29 says, "Otherwise, he might complete only the foundation before running out of funds." Prayerfully plan ahead as you revise your budget.

3. *Restrict.* Set a goal to restrict your spending and the use of your credit cards. This is a familiar and dangerous trap that most people fall into, spending more than they are making brought on by charging things "on sale" they cannot afford. Highly motivated marketing and advertising makes it so enticing to buy, buy, buy and just charge it. It gives the impression

that you can buy all you want now and pay for it later—and pay, you do. Most people are unaware of the high interest rates per month, and you end up paying about one third more than the sale price you paid for it. It may be time to have "plastic surgery" and cut up most of your credit cards, keeping only one or two for emergency purposes and buying only what you can afford to pay off at the end of the month.

Restrict your spending and stay within your revised budget. We need to carefully watch that our material possessions do not become an obsession. Remember, we must all give an accounting to God, so we want to be wise with *His* money, setting a good example for your family.

4. *Recoup*. After you get yourself on a budget and restrict your spending, then try and recoup your losses and take care of your debts. We need to seriously work toward being debt-free except for our home mortgages. How can this be done? By staying on your budget and stop spending more than you are earning. You need to find creative ways to save money and begin cutting back in all areas.

One of the biggest area is food costs. Shop wisely, check for sales especially two-for-one specials, use store coupons, and go where they give doubles. Caution: don't buy just because you have a coupon. Buy only what you need. Understand unit prices and pricing per pound. Check on co-op buying. This is wonderful for large families. Learn how to prepare easy, cost-saving recipes.

Watch for bargains in every area, not just at the grocery store. Check out the thrift stores and bargain basements. Don't miss garage sales, especially for children's clothes or baby items. The consignment stores are great for women's and children's clothes too. In fact, bring your old clothes in that don't fit anymore and have them sold on consignment. That way, you can earn money to buy reruns for yourself and your family. Have a clothing exchange at your church or school. This is a wonderful way to help the needy, and especially single moms and young parents.

A co-op babysitting is a good way to help one another. This can be set up through your church, or even in your neighborhood. Bill and I recommend this highly for couples. This way, they can date on a regular basis. One couple babysitting for the other. They can save the expense of a babysitter and still go out. This works so well with the young moms when they have to go to the doctor's office, shopping, or just out for the day. We need to get back to the bartering system, using your gifts and talents to help one another. I cut my girlfriend's hair in exchange for vitamins. This works out well for both of us. Or you could sew in exchange for baked goods. There are so many more creative ideas. These are just a few to help you see how you can be a part of the plan and process of getting out of debt.

Being a homemaker is wonderful. You can be a vital part of the family income without going outside the home. For those who have chosen to work outside of the home, you can still be a part of these co-op opportunities while supplementing your income to get out of debt. As this is being done, you are laying the foundation of financial freedom and the foundation of a secure family life.

5. *Rebuild.* With your newfound *resources* and *revising* your budget, *restricting* your spending and *recouping* your debts, you are now ready to *rebuild* your lives starting with your family. Financial problems are known to be one of the main causes of family conflict. We do need to recognize it as the problem and not blame or condemn your spouse for past mistakes and bad investments. We all need advice and instruction in this area. When we get it, then we both need to agree on a reasonable plan and be committed to work it out together, agreeing

"wholeheartedly with one another." With God's plan and His blueprints, you *can* begin to rebuild your family's relationships.

Begin in a practical way—by spending quality time together that fits the budget. Do things that let you get to know each other in a more intimate way. Starting with your spouse, have a date night, just the two of you. It doesn't have to be expensive: McDonald's, a picnic, or even a drive to a quiet spot where you can give each other undivided attention. This says, "You are important to me. I love you."

The same with your children. It has been said that the average father spends approximately thirty-seven minutes a week with his child. This is outrageous but true. Your children need to know they are important to you. Take the time to be alone with each one and then as a family. Have fun together. This is so essential in rebuilding relationships. It is especially true with our relationship with the Lord, which brings us to point number 6.

6. *Return*. Yes, we need to return to our Source of hope and help—the Lord. He does want first place in our lives. We need to *renew* our commitment to him and *rebuild* our relationship with Him. You need to trust Him with your life and to meet your needs according to His riches in glory, not your own resources. We all need to put Him first, our family next, then our future, and then our finances. When everything is in the right order, you can then faithfully work together toward your goals of having a firm family foundation and being financially free.

God's plan must be in order if we are to have marital compatibility and financial stability. The place to be is to *return* to your First Love—the Lord Jesus Christ—and then *all* things *will* be added to you. It can be done; start today! "We *can* do *all* things through Christ who gives us the strength" (Phil. 4:13, emphasis added).

Chapter 8

Let's Replace Fear for Faith

Anyone afraid of flying? Hang-on and come fly with me through this chapter on fear! It was March of 1983 in Florida. Bill and I had just completed a weekend conference for the company we were working with at the time. We were preparing to fly back to Memphis. I had arrived on Friday and had flown on a commercial airline while all of the others traveled on the company plane. They were going home on that same small company plane, but I was *determined* not to and had, in fact, already called the airlines to see what options were available. Much to my dismay, there was not one seat available on any of the three airlines I called. It was stand-by only, and the cost was $232.00 one way. I was shocked at the price, but thought my life is certainly worth $232.00, isn't it? I was not going to fly on that small plane. I had a hard enough time getting on a large one.

Fear? Oh *no*. Christians are not supposed to have fears, are we? Besides, I rationalized my feelings by making a list of the reasons why my decision was valid:

1. I do not like to fly. Period. (Now, I'm not afraid to die, just fly!)

2. I get motion sickness.
3. I did not like the idea of me and Bill being on the same small airplane. What if something happened to both of us? Who would take care of the children?
4. The biggest reason was the weather. The morning report was bad: storms and tornadoes in Northern Florida and Alabama and bad weather in Memphis—the exact route we had to take.

Oh no, I thought. *I'm not going to be in a small plane going through storms. Nope, not me. That's it! I'm not going! I'll go stand-by and meet you there.* We continued to discuss it through lunch, and everyone was so surprised that this lady of "great faith" sounded "fearful." I still would not admit to my fear because I had all of these logical reasons that sounded good to me. As the hour passed, my reasons were diminishing.

1. I did believe my life was in the Lord's hands, and the Bible says, "Fear not, I will be with you." Okay, I agreed to that. That's what I preached to others and now I had to practice what I preached.
2. Bill had bought me some powerful motion sickness pills. That should take care of that!
3. Bill said not to worry about us flying together. Our wills had been prepared, and the kids would be well taken care of. I *really* didn't like that answer, but it gave me a little assurance.
4. The weather had improved, and we were cleared to take off in an hour. Darn! All of my reasons were "flying away!"

We had to go back up to our rooms to get our luggage. I was still struggling. I was literally on my knees, praying for peace, but it wouldn't come because I was hanging on for dear life. I would not let go of the controls and let God take over! I remember thinking, *Okay, Lord. I'm going to call the airlines once more. If there is not a seat open, Lord, I'll know that You want me on the company plane.* "Aren't we funny the way we bargain with God? "If *You* do this for me, Lord, I'll do *this* for you." Well, I could not even get through to the airlines because the phone lines were busy.

Bill said, "I can't even imagine you wanting to spend $232 when we have a private plane at our disposal." He said, "Jeannie, come on. You'll love it."

Don't you just hate when someone tells you what you will like? I knew I wouldn't, but all of my resources and excuses had run out; and by then, everyone was waiting in the hotel lobby for us. I faked a big smile to cover my fear, and we all got into a cab—six of us and sixteen pieces of luggage! We laughed and joked, and tried to keep it light as we drove to the airport.

When we arrived, I could see the commercial airport in the distance and all of those big jets. Then I looked at all of the rows of private planes. The rows began with the larger ones first. We drove up and down the rows, and we couldn't find the plane!

Good! I thought. *Maybe someone stole it!* Of course, that wasn't true, but it was a good thought! You must understand, I had never seen this plane before, so I did not know how big or small it was. As the rows increased, the planes decreased in size.

Oh no, I thought. *Now I know why I hadn't seen the plane before.* The lump in my throat tightened. I couldn't even talk, something unheard of for *me!*

We approached this teeny, tiny, little, I mean, *small*, *single*-engine (meaning one) Saratoga. The knot in my stomach got bigger and bigger as the planes got smaller and smaller. *One engine*, I thought. *No back up. What if… Oh my!* My knees got weak as I got out of the cab, which looked bigger than the inside of the plane at that point. My vision narrowed as the plane did look smaller than the cab. I thought. *How are they going to get all sixteen pieces of luggage, much less all of us, on that plane?* My mind was racing. My eyes looked far in the distance, and just across a "big" fence was the "big" airport. I envisioned myself running and taking a quantum leap over the fence and boarding any plane out of there! I thought, *Lord, Lord, the battle is on again!* What was it going to take to win this one?

As they began loading the plane with all of that luggage, I thought my problems were over. I was sure we would never get off the ground with all the weight we were carrying. I remember thinking, *I wish I would have lost these ten pounds before I came, as if that would help!* Actually, I thought maybe it would and offered to stay behind so we wouldn't be over our flying weight. We were almost loaded when they realized they had left the keys for the plane at the terminal and asked Bill to go back and get them!

This was it! My last chance to escape! I grabbed my jacket and ran with Bill back to the terminal. The lady at the desk saw me gasping for breath and turning gray very quickly. She saw my fear and said, "I don't blame you. I don't like to fly in small planes, either. I got deathly sick on my first flight!"

With that, I panicked and went into the ladies' room to splash myself with cold water because I actually thought I was going to faint! I looked at myself in the mirror, and I didn't even recognize myself. Fear had overpowered me.

I cried out to God once more and said, "Please, Lord. Please take away my fear and replace it with faith—faith in You. I know You love me, and I know my life is in Your hands. Okay, Lord. I give this area of my life to you. You take over. I surrender my fear and control to You. Fill me with Your peace as I exchange fear with faith." You see, I'm not saying it is easy, but I am saying it can be done. It is determined by how long or tight we hang on. Well, I let go totally and completely (I did take two more Dramamine), and came out of the ladies' room a different person (well, better than when I went in).

Anyway, I walked calmly and confidently with Bill back to the plane. He helped me up on the wing (that's the way you had to get into this plane). Everyone stood and watched as I put my two feet in the water, oops, I mean the plane. Yes, I did feel like I was at the edge of the Red Sea and God waited until I took the first step of faith and then, just as He parted the Sea, He gave me peace. Yes, His peace that passes *all* understanding.

They let me sit in the front, thinking it would be smoother for me. As I looked at all of those gadgets, instruments, and controls, I quickly remembered Who was in control. I was clutching my Bible for the take-off, thinking if I was going to die, I wanted my Bible in my hand!

Seriously, as we were smoothly creeping up to two thousand feet, I opened my Bible to Psalm 19:1, "The heavens declare the glory of God. They are a marvelous display of His handiwork," and that it was as soft clouds billowed around. The sky was blue and the sun was shining. Oh my! What a glorious sight! I also read Psalm 91 during the flight and was enlightened and comforted by these verses: "*He* will shield you with *His* wings. [I didn't have to depend on the plane's wings]. *He* is my place of safety" (v. 4); "You don't need to *fear* the dangers of the day or the disaster of the morning" (v. 5); and "For *He* orders *His* angels to protect you wherever you go" (v. 11, emphasis added). I could almost feel the angel wings of protection. My fear was gone, and I praised Him for these promises!

Does this mean I never had fear again? Oh no. This was a great victory for me, but fear has many faces and finds you in different places. How we deal with each one helps us to be strong for the next time. Here are some ways to have *Hope for the Days Ahead* in your times of fear.

Fear brings on confusion and virtually makes it impossible to concentrate on the things of God. When a *negative* thought comes into our minds, we need to replace it with a *positive* promise. I am so thankful that God has given us many promises for all types of fear:

- For *confusion*, we can have *confidence* in Him. "I have not given you a spirit of fear, but of *love* and a *sound mind*" (2 Tim. 1:7, emphasis added).
- For *abandonment*: "I will be with you. I will not abandon you. I will never leave you or forsake you" (Heb. 13:5)
- For *help*: "I will not be afraid because the Lord is my *Helper*" (Heb. 13:6, emphasis added)
- For *finances*: "I will supply all of your needs from *My riches* in glory" (Phil. 4:19, emphasis added)
- For *death*: "I am the Resurrection and the *Life*. He who is in Me shall never die" (John 11:25, emphasis added).
- For *heights* and *water*: "If I take the wings of the morning or dwell in the uttermost parts of the sea, even there, You shall lead me and Your hand holds me" (Ps. 139:19–10)
- For *darkness*: "Even the darkness hides nothing from You. The *night shines as the day*—the darkness and light are both alike to You" (Ps. 139: 9–10, emphasis added).

There are different types of fears and levels of fear, but they are all real and need to be dealt with.

There are fears relating to your family, future and finances, loss of a job, facing bankruptcy, losing your home or child, children gone astray or who have run away or living an abnormal, immoral lifestyle, abuse, rejection, abandonment, mistakes in a bad decision or business, failures, or even death due to sickness such as an incurable disease or an accident, or maybe your future looks bleak.

These all bring on a fear of the unknown. *Where will I go? What will I do?*

Yes, it is very hard to trust at a time like this and turn our lives over to an all-knowing God. Fear definitely is not funny—it's frightening! There are times when things seem completely out of control and we feel that gripping siege of fear. There are times when we wonder for a moment, or longer, days, maybe weeks: *does God really care? Does He know and understand the deepest fears of our hearts?*

As soon as we let that doubt enter our minds, our emotions take over and give in to the lies and deception of the enemy. When we start doubting the power of God, it brings on anxiety and completely paralyzes our mind.

If God makes a promise (and He has) to meet our needs, we don't have to be anxious. The antidote for anxiety is *abide*. John 15:3 states, "Abide in Me and I will abide in you." Verse 7 says, "If you abide in Me and My Words remain in you, ask whatever you will and it will be done for you." When we surrender all to Him and *abide* in Him, this means we are accepting His sovereignty, believing His will and plan for us is best. We are giving over the control of our lives, placing our confidence in Christ to take care of everything that concerns us.

This does not mean that we can sit back and not take responsibility, but our first responsibility is to lay our burdens before the Lord and leave them there. Psalm 55:22 states, "Give your burdens to the Lord. He will carry them." I know we are inclined to pick them up again. This is a process but one that you can have victory in as you continue to give God control of every area of your life. Psalm 125:1 says, "Those who trust in the Lord are unmoved by any circumstance."

I know one thing for sure: God does not want us to be paralyzed with fear. Nor does He want us to take control of our circumstances. He wants us to remember and surrender. Remember, God is the Blessed Controller of *all* things. God wants us to completely surrender everything to Him. God does not want us to struggle or try to figure out a solution. The problems we face may be legitimate concerns, but God wants you to trust Him to work in your life so you can experience the blessings of His power and promises. Fear, carried to extreme, is frustration and brings anxiety and feelings of failure and fretfulness. The Bible tells us very clearly in Philippians 4:6–7, "Be *anxious* for nothing, but in *everything*, by prayer and supplication with thanksgiving, let your requests be made known to God and the *peace* of God which surpasses all comprehension *shall* guard your hearts and your minds in Christ Jesus" (emphasis added).

Is this easy? No!

We do need help, and Jesus told us in His Word that His help for us is the Holy Spirit in John 15:20. "I will send you a Comforter and He will guide you into all truth and the truth will set you free." Yes, you can be free—free from the power of fear through faith. Faith in a God who loves you and who is faithful even when we are not. Through this freeing faith, ask Him to help you, heal you from your worries and fears. Resist the enemy's tricks to take your joy away. His lies will keep you in bondage. Place your confidence in Christ and His powerful promises. The truth is what God says, no matter how you feel.

Find a godly woman who will stand with you, encourage you, pray for you, and who will remind you of His promises; someone who will help you to keep your focus on Christ and not your fear or circumstances. I have had many women like this through my Christian life and wouldn't be where I am today without them. Then in turn, as I do, you will be able to impart these truths to others with a positive faith and trust in a powerful God who loves us. He knew that we would have fear come into our lives. Did you know that he loves us so much that there are 365 "fear not's" in the Bible? One for each day in a year. Let me end with this scriptural promise: "Be strong and courageous. Do not be afraid for the Lord your God will be with you. He will not forsake you" (Deut. 31:6).

Chapter 9

Lord, I Need a Friend Like You with Arms to Hug Me

I believe one of the greatest needs we all have is that of a good friend. When I began writing this chapter, I asked several people from all walks of life and all ages to tell me what friendship meant to them, and to give me a definition of a true friend. I found it means many things to many people. These are a few. See if you can relate to some of them.

A friend is someone who:

- listens and never turns their back on you or judges you;
- loves you and accepts you just as you are unconditionally;
- understands that you are not perfect;
- drops everything they are doing to talk to you, is always there to help you;
- watches your children when you are in a pinch or picks them up from school;
- takes you to an appointment when you don't have a car;
- lends you her clothes or jewelry for special occasions;

- makes chicken soup when you are sick;
- says, "Come on in and be yourself";
- is sensitive to your needs, will pray with you and for you, and encourage you;
- doesn't put unrealistic expectations on you;
- is not jealous and only wants the best for you;
- is honest when it matters;
- Someone you can trust;is in tune with you and sensitive to your needs;
- gives you the help you need, not the help they think you need;
- it is someone who we tell our innermost secrets;
- knows that true friendship, like love, can spark at any age;
- believes that true friendship requires a certain level of maturity and mutual understanding;
- knows instinctively when to be available and when to let you be alone;
- knows that sometimes, lives touch very deeply, but only for a short period of time. That does not diminish that friendship.

Friends show they care by just being there. Friendship is a matter of the heart. It is giving and receiving, sharing and caring, laughing, crying, being honest and transparent, free to be, and say who and what you are with no pretenses. A friendship is built on transparency, honesty, confrontation, support, accountability, warmth, and a prayerful concern through life's ups and downs. It is practical and spiritual. We all need each other. We all need friends as our needs vary and lives change. We need new and different friends based on where we are in life's circumstances. The Lord always supplies these needs at the right time.

Yes, friendship is all of these and more. We need to look at this in light of not only finding a friend who will meet only your needs and be a friend, but asks, "How can I be that true friend?" If we want a friend, we need to sow seeds of friendship. How can we do that? By understanding just what friendship is.

In doing the research for this chapter, it was revealed to me in a new and deeper way just what a friendship is. As a result, I was able to realize and understand more clearly that there are *many* different types of friendships. With that, I was able to reevaluate the commitment that goes along with a friendship. This helped me to recognize that we need to identify the purpose of our friendships and realize again that not all friendships are the same. This led me to reflect on my past friendships and review how I acted and reacted as a friend through the years and in the different stages of my life. It was quite revealing, and as a result, I have been able to reconcile and restore one of my first and longtime friendships. I trust this chapter will be helpful to you as we research this precious word—"friendship."

Let's begin with looking at all of the positive words that come to mind when we think of a good friend. Keep in mind now that there are different kinds and levels of friendship.

First, let's accentuate the positive. When I think of words that describe a *true* friend, they are faithful, forgiving, freeing, fun, loyal, listening, understanding, uplifting, encouraging, inspiring, praying, accepting, available, considerate, courteous, caring, kind, reliable, helpful, trustworthy, and honest.

Looking at these descriptive words, we know that only Jesus can be that kind of friend. He is all of these and much more. He loves us and accepts us, not for what we do, but for who we are. He will never fail us or leave us, and He does stick closer than a brother. We know that in our heart and spirit and even our mind, but I have heard so many people say, "I need someone like Jesus with arms to hug me." In our darkest hour, when we are grieved by sorrow, anguished by pain, paralyzed with fear, when our heart hurts so badly we cannot even process it in our minds and it actually affects every area of our body, yes, we know Jesus is there in Spirit and in truth.

But we need someone we can see, look at, feel, touch, hang on to, collapse in their arms if need be. Someone who will reach out and hug us, care for us, listen to us, cry with us, or just be there to comfort and support us in loving care and faithful prayer. I heard a song on the radio once. I don't even know the name of it, but the chorus had words like this: "I'll stand by you when you need a helping hand. I'll stand by you. I'll be your friend who understands. I'll be your shoulder to lean on. I'll stand by you." Yes, we all need this type of true friend. If you have a friend like this, you are very fortunate as they are definitely heaven-sent.

All friendships are different. We are describing a true, godly friend in this chapter, almost one of a kind or maybe a few with a mixture of qualities. As we look at the facets of friendship, let's not only focus on what we need in a friend or from a friend, but also on what kind of friend we can be to someone else.

It is interesting to note that our English word "friend" comes from the same root word as "free." Yes, a true friend lets us "be free to be me," as the saying goes. Free to be who and what we are. Free to be different, to have different ideas, views, beliefs, and free to express them even if we don't agree. Yes, a true friend can disagree and still love at the same time.

That brings us to a *faithful* friend. This is someone who is always there for you no matter what we say or do, through thick or thin, good times and bad, they will stand by you faithfully to the end. This person will also be a *loyal* friend—one who will be your confidante, one you can tell anything to and they will never betray you. They can be trusted with your most intimate thoughts. They will be trustworthy and true. A friend who is *kind*, *considerate*, and *caring*. Someone who will put you first, consider your needs before theirs, will be courteous and kind in their actions, caring for you in a loving way.

A friend who is *helpful* is usually always *available*. One who will set aside their tasks and make time for you. They will put you first, think of you first, and be available to help you both physically and emotionally.

A friend will also have *understanding*, discernment, and insight. One who probably has been where you are and can relate to your needs with an empathetic heart. They will have a listening heart. One who "listens in love" and does not presume, assume, condemn, or judge you. Someone who lets you share your deepest hurts and can let you express your innermost feelings.

A reliable friend is one you can depend on to be responsible, on time, credible—the all-around, secure, and stable person you need especially in times of crisis and uncertainties.

Then there are times when you need a *fun-loving* friend—one with whom you can be carefree, have a good time, and even be silly. One who will help you take your mind off your problems and make you laugh because laughter is freeing, like a good medicine. We all need friends who are *uplifting, inspiring,* and *encouraging*. One who will *lift* your spirit and *inspire* you to turn to your Source of hope—the Lord (Psalm 39:7 states, "Lord, my only hope is in You!"), and *encourage* you to go on and assure you they will be there to help you through it. First Thessalonians 5:11–14 says, "Encourage the faint-hearted, help the weak and be patient with all men."

Oh yes, the *patient* friend. This is one we need desperately. One who will "have the patience of a saint," as they say. One who never gets tired of hearing our woes and cares, who very gently and patiently endures with us over and over as long as it takes.

Then, of course, there is that *forgiving* friend. This friend is one who harbors no grudges even if we frustrate or fail them; they are faithful to forgive. They overlook with compassion, not condemnation. Colossians 3:13 says, "Bearing with one another and forgiving each other just as the Lord forgave you."

And our *prayerful* friends—those close by and far away. Those dear, precious prayer partners of ours that we can call and say, "Pray for me, cover me. I cannot even pray today. I'm in so much pain." The ones who prayerfully intercede on your behalf. The ones who do not even have to know what the details of your requests are, they just faithfully pray. "Bear ye one another's burdens." "The prayers of a righteous man availeth much" (Gal. 6:2).

Then there is that friend who loves like Jesus loves. A *loving* friend who sets no boundaries, no limits, no conditions. One who loves unconditionally no matter what we do or say. A loving friend is all of these in one—unique, special, one-of-a-kind relationship. If you have a friend like this, you are truly blessed.

I have this kind of friend, and her name is Rita Bruno. She is and does have all of these qualities as a friend. She has been my dear and longtime friend, and her feelings for me through the years have never changed. She is a true friend to many and carries the Christ-like qualities in her relationships. I feel privileged to have this special gift of a true friend. Through all of our thirty-plus years, our mutual understanding and love has remained the same even though the miles separated us and time passed on. Even when we did not write or call for a while, when we spoke, we just picked up where we left off. No excuses, no guilt if we missed a birthday card or two, because our friendship goes beyond doing. It is based on just being there in spirit and a bond of love.

When Rita came from Georgia to California for my fiftieth birthday, she made this statement that touched the depth of my heart. She said our friendship is like Jesus—unconditional and sacrificial, and yes, she would actually give up her life for me. John 15:13 says, "The greatest love is shown when a person lays down his life for his friend." Now that is a true friend! Thank you, Rita, for being my friend, and I want you to know the feeling is mutual. You are a friend like Jesus to me.

We have looked at all the positive qualities; we realize Jesus is the only one who can be all of these to us at all times. None of us will be able to portray that pure perfection as He can. But I do feel we need to be aware of our responsibility as a friend. People do need to see Jesus in us through His life in us so they can be drawn closer to Jesus.

I know this is what happened in my life. I saw Jesus's love in so many friends—the heaven-sent ones. I have to say, I have had the privilege of having many through the years. I know I would not be where I am today if it were not for their example of unconditional love, constant care, powerful prayers, and faithful friendships. I remember thanking the Lord over and over for each person He brought into my life at just the right time. I asked him to give me the compassion, understanding, sensitivity, wisdom, and strength to be the same kind of friend. I wanted to be able to minister this love and care, and let people see not me, but Jesus's life and Spirit in me. I wanted to be that friend like Jesus, with arms to hug them and be there for them as so many were there for me.

Although this has been my heart's desire, I have not on every occasion or circumstance been able to be all that people needed me to be. Yes, as the Bible says, no one is perfect. We all fall short, and we have feet of clay. Yes, we do fail. Not intentionally, but it does happen. But oh, to know the freeing balm of forgiveness. To know that He is faithful to forgive us and with that, we have the freedom to forgive and go on in our friendships.

There are many different kinds of friendships. Childhood friends are so important because they were our first friends. We called them playmates, and they were usually from our neighborhood, schools, or churches we attended. We also had schoolmates and began building more solid relationships by grade school, and carried them on into junior and senior high school. These were good friends, and we still have many of them today. Some moved away and made new friends, and some went off to college and had roommates who became good friends. Others went on to pursue a career and had coworkers, associates, and colleagues as friends. These types of friends were all significant at different levels and served a different purpose at the time.

When we got married, our friendships took on a different meaning. In most cases, our husbands became our best friends. Now I know that is not always the case, but it is the ideal, and sometimes, we have to work at getting it to that point because after Jesus, your husband should be your closest friend. I know it can be done as Bill and I are best friends. Once we found the Lord, got our priorities in order, and put each other's needs first, we did become the best of friends. I praise the Lord for what He has done in our life and for the intimate, trusting, loving, and understanding relationship we have at this time.

We have now looked at several different types of friendships ranging from childhood playmates to college roommates to our mates, if we are married. Do you see how our circumstances change and how we have to *reevaluate* our commitment in our friendships to coincide with our circumstances?

For instance, college roommates and friends from work: these are very special, deep friendships. But what happens when one gets married, or leaves that job and cannot be the same kind of friend? That friendship takes on a new meaning and different responsibility. The married person has to divide her time and attention, and cannot give the single person the quantity of time and complete attention as they did before. This is hard for both and really needs to be handled in a very tender way, or there will be misunderstanding and feelings of rejection. If this isn't discussed and decided on beforehand, it may cause a terrible strain in the friendship.

This is equally as hard for the married person as it is for the single one. One is trying to adjust to being with someone; and the other is feeling lonely, rejected, and sometimes jealous because they are alone. It is almost a bittersweet situation. Mutual understanding and preset boundaries need to be established such as setting aside time to be together when it does not conflict with the couple's schedule, or having a time to call on the phone when it will not interfere with the single's schedule. Plan lunches and coffee times to talk and catch up, and keep that relationship going. Being sensitive to both party's needs and understanding they will be different than before. It must be understood that the friendship is taking on a new responsibility, and it will continue to do so and become more complicated as the years go by especially when they start to have children. Then, not only is their time, attention, and energy stretched in more directions, but you find you cannot even relate anymore as your interests have changed and you have less in common. I have seen this happen to so many good friendships, and it really doesn't have to if we recognize this ahead of time. If it has happened to you, I recommend you prayerfully make an attempt to reconcile.

Friendship is stretched again and is very difficult especially when people move away after you have established so many good, solid friendships. You are used to just calling someone for a shoulder to cry on or need someone to pray with, some comfort, or caring person to be with. You may just need someone to say, "Let's drop everything and go shopping." Yes, this is a very difficult adjustment. Long distance love is not easy.

I remember just sharing these thoughts with some dear friends, Gwen, Delores, Julie, and Sandy, pals of mine from Illinois. We established that our love and commitment for one another has not changed through the years, but things have changed. Our circumstances have caused us to be separated, so we may not be able to be there physically in friendship. This is very hard to adjust to especially if you are going through a crisis, which most of us do at some point in our lives. We need that deep bond of friendship we once had to help get us through. That is why it is so important for us to commit to being that kind of friend to someone even if it is long-distance love through prayer, calls, and notes. Let them know you still care.

Everywhere we have moved, God has replaced our friends. Not in the sense of taking their *place* but replacing them to fill that need that we have. God's care can be felt across the miles.

I remember when we first moved to Atlanta. The staff at Grace Ministries were gracious in so many ways. They brought house warming gifts, invited us to their homes, out for dinners and to visit their Churches. Many others were there in loving support with calls and prayers saying, "we're here if you need us." We felt welcomed by everyone. Patti Randell Jacobson picked me up for Bible study every Wednesday. It was exactly what I needed, to study God's Word and meet new friends. We developed a close friendship and were there for each other in many prayerful and practical ways. When Patty needed someone to pick her son Stephen after school, I was available. When I needed a dressy dress and jewelry for a formal occasion she would lend me hers and does so even to this day. We still remain long-distance faithful friends, what a blessing to have friends like these. We appreciated all of them.

Do you see how important the practical things are? That is what Jesus does all the time. He provides what we need through His people. Therefore, we need to be sensitive with new people who move into our area and decide what kind of friend you are going to be. Some of you will bake a cake while others will bring over a cooked meal. Maybe invite them over for a casual meal or dessert. Some of you may make yourself available to take them to a Doctor's appointment or watch their children when needed. After you get to know them, you may invite them to your church or Bible study. Remember, these are different from other friendships you may have, but these do require a real commitment.

After we reevaluate our gifts, we also have to realize that it may take on a new level of commitment, and we may have to reconsider our role in certain *relationships*, perhaps replacing them with less restrictions and requirements. Again, this needs to be done in a prayerful, agreeable manner. The next big step is to *realize* also that we just cannot be all things to all people. We really need to ask the Lord to *reveal* these to us, and after we *recognize* what they are, ask Him to lead and guide you as to what your role can be in specific friendships. Otherwise, we will disappoint and fail that person who is expecting something from us that we cannot give. As a result, we will feel guilty and feel like we failed them.

We also have to remember we cannot do this with and in our own *resources*. We do need to do it in His strength and power. First Corinthians 12:4 says, "We all have different gifts and abilities but it's the same God through the Holy Spirit who gives us the power to do them all." When we recognize what our gifts are, then we can freely and comfortably establish our role in certain relationships and extend the type of friendship a person needs. Not from our resources, but from God's.

With these truths revealed as our foundation, we can then set reasonable boundaries in certain relationships and have the freedom to function within them, protecting us from hard feelings, disappointments, and misunderstood feelings when unrealistic expectations are not met.

I think of how effectively this can work in a church situation when each person is using their gifts properly. When a person is in need, many people will have a specific part in that person's life. Many friends, if you will, will be the support group during their time of crisis. One may be a prayer warrior and will stand with them in prayer. One could be practical and give good, sound advice. One will be straightforward and have the freedom to confront in love. One may volunteer to do research and find resource material like books and CDs for them to read and listen. One friend may have wisdom, discernment, and understanding, and will be their counselor and give them Godly advice. One will just listen and let them share openly. Altogether, they become that special friend to the person at that time.

You see how important it is to recognize your gifts and what commitment you can comfortably make in different situations and relationships. We all need each other to complete the work of the body of Christ, each one with a different gift and knowing what it is. After all of this has been revealed, you can do as I did and reflect back on your friendships and see if there are any you need to restore. Let me share with you what happened to me.

I actually called my very first friend in life with the intention of asking her to remember all of the good things about our friendship. I had just started to write this chapter, and I was excited about the fond memories we could reminisce about.

Much to my surprise, when I asked her to write down some thoughts about our friendship, she hesitated and said, "I'm not sure you will want to hear what I have to say."

Oh my, I thought as I heard the hurt in her voice. *What could she mean? What have I done?* In the next breath, I was quick to say, "Lois, you were my very first friend. You have a special place in my heart and always will. My feelings for you have never changed."

"Yes, that may be true," she said. "But nonetheless, through the years, you have done some things that hurt and offended me."

Do we hurt our friends? Do we reject them? Do we disappoint or judge them? Or maybe take advantage of them and take them for granted? Unfortunately, yes. But intentionally? No.

Nonetheless, we need to *realize* that perhaps, we unknowingly did hurt a friend along the way. That is why it is so good to not only *reflect* on your past friendships, but also ask the Lord to *reveal* the truths to you, and then we need to take the next step and *reconcile* these *relationships* and *restore* the friendships. The Bible not only tells us to love one another but to forgive one another as Christ loves and forgives us. Lois and I have dealt with all of our past issues. I humbly asked for forgiveness for offending her. It wasn't intentional, but nonetheless, she was hurt. I needed to restore and reconcile our relationship, and I did. We *realized* we were young and immature, thinking of our own needs and putting unrealistic expectations on our relationship. We found out that you cannot demand or expect your friends to be what you need them to be at certain times. Because when they cannot be that for you, you feel rejected and unaccepted, unloved, and even sometimes betrayed as a friend. Much of this has to do with our maturity level and not understanding where the other person is coming from intellectually, emotionally, and spiritually at that time.

That's why in close friendships, we have to be so sensitive to the other's needs and emotions. As we reflected on some specific incidents in our past relationship, we could see how that happened. Now we can look at it in a different light, but at the time, it was hurtful and caused resentment. Our words of advice to close friends who are feeling this way and carrying hurtful thoughts and hard feelings are to please prayerfully *reflect* on your past relationships, be honest with each other, and *reveal* any past hurts known or unknown. *Reconcile* by sincerely asking for forgiveness for these offenses, as I did, and then *restore* your relationship to where it should be—forever friends. We did, and it was a great feeling. We both felt free—free to be me, free to be friends. Thanks, Lois, for being my very first and longtime friend. Thank you for being bold enough to confront me with my offenses. I do thank the Lord for the renewed friendship we have.

In fact, Lois gave me the title for this chapter. It keeps growing closer and deeper each year!

I want to thank another friend, Marcy, who played in an intricate part in this friendship. She was a friend to both Lois and me; and through the years, she sensed the strain, hurt, and rejection. It was through her sensitive and consistent spirit that brought us together so we could sort this through and reconcile. You see how important it is to have many friends who play a different role in our lives, each with a different gift and sense of insight. Marcy saw the whole picture from both sides and knew we needed to be brought together in love, honesty, forgiveness, and reconciliation. Thanks, Marcy, for being that kind of friend. You are very dear to me and have been a longtime and faithful friend to both of us. What's so great is that now, in our later years, we, along with our husbands, can all enjoy each other's company as couples with no hang ups from the past. Lois and Dick, Marcy and Jack, Ducky and Jani, and Bill and I are free to have fun and enjoy our friendships to the fullest! We have looked at the positive aspects of friendship and even looked at some of the negative ones with the conclusion of forgiveness, reconciliation, and restoration. Now let's look at another aspect.

What about the person who has no friends? There are many in this world, *unfortunately*, and they live right in our neighborhood, churches, schools, and workplaces. What do you do when you do not have a close friend or even a family or support group? What about when you have rejection at work and your husband isn't your best friend, and you have no children or grandchildren to divert your attention to?

So let's look at those who are friendless. They are so lonely. They feel isolated, rejected—almost abandoned and forsaken to the point of feeling unwanted, unliked, and even unwelcomed at times. Think of this person who has no one to turn to, to talk to, to cry with, laugh with, to just be herself. Then take it a step further and picture them in a crisis situation with no one there to support them, hug them, and help them. Yes, there are many people like this.

Will Jesus be enough for them? Yes, spiritually and eternally. His promises do give us hope. But emotionally and physically, the friendless need someone like Jesus with arms to hug them, to encourage them, and to comfort them. This is where we come in. How can we be that kind of friend, or how can we be instrumental in starting a friendship group?

We need to begin with prayer and ask God to lead us in this type of ministry if that is what His plan is for you. I believe it can be done simply and very effectively, one-on-one or on a small scale. You can ask the Lord to give you one person to befriend, whether it be at work, school, or in your neighborhood. Review all the *R* points in this chapter and remember to only commit to what you are gifted in and rely on the Lord's help in being the type of friend that person needs.

If the Lord gives you a larger vision of starting a small friendship group in your home, then proceed as He directs, keeping it simple so as not to intimidate anyone or make them feel uncomfortable. This will not be a counseling session or a gossip session, but rather a time of bonding in a caring way. See what the needs are and keep all sharing prayerful and confidential. You will probably see this expand to greater needs, and if so, please get under the direction and support of your church and/or women's ministry group. This is not to be a Bible study at this point. It may develop into that and those that wish to will progress into that commitment. The larger aspect of that is an actual *care* group or friendship group at your church. This definitely should be under the direction of the women's ministry, or another small-group ministry, to keep the focus on the needs of the women. There are many good books available for deeper insight and direction at your local Christian bookstore.

We need to be a friend to someone like Jesus with arms to hug them. In order to do that, we have to know the only One who can be the friend we need when we have received Jesus into our life and have experienced His life in us. Then and only then can we reflect that love—His love—to others. The Bible tells us in John 13:34–35, "A new commandment I give to you—that you love one another as I have loved you."

When we take the focus off our needs, we are free to love like Jesus loves—unconditionally with a total acceptance without expecting anything in return. That way, we are not expecting someone to be what only Jesus Christ can be in our lives—our closest, dearest friend. When we have established this as our foundation and security, then and only then can we be a faithful friend to someone else. This type of friendship takes (1) submission to God, (2) sacrifice to self, and (3) unconditional love for others. Proverbs 17:7 says, "A true friend, however, loves at all times." And Proverbs 18:24 states, "There is a friend that sticks closer than a brother." May I encourage you to be that kind of friend to someone, the kind with "arms to hug them."

Because I have had so many dear and faithful friends through the years, I would need to write another book just to include all of their names. So as my tribute to each one of them, I have written a poem where each one will find their names woven through the lines. Please know that you will always be written on and woven in my heart. Thank you and God bless you all.

A Poem for My Friends

You have been my friend right from the start,
You have a special place in my heart.
You were there during my growing up years,
We shared much laughter and some tears.
We all fell in love and got married,
A new dimension our friendship carried.
Then came children and a new responsibility,
Our friendships were changing, we could see.
Some of us began to move away,
Yes, we were sad on that day.
But we faithfully kept in touch,
With those friends we loved so much.
Our classmates would gather at our reunion,
It was great to see what everyone was doing.
Our lives were changing again and again,
It was fun to reminisce what happened back then.
Thank you, friends, for the memories,
Now as we grow old, we can cherish these.
For those we have met in other places,
I thank the Lord too for your faces.
God knew what I needed for each time,
And intertwined your life with mine.

LORD, I NEED A FRIEND LIKE YOU WITH ARMS TO HUG ME

Many have stood by us, through thick and thin,
And helped as a new life we did begin.
Dear friends, you see,
You have meant so very much to me,
Each one has met a specific need.
Some taught me how to study God's Word,
Others helped me to share what I had heard.
For those whose wisdom and advice I do treasure,
I will be humbly grateful to you forever.
Those who have been faithful in loving care,
Always there to share in a prayer.
At times, it was not easy to explain,
Or times when I was in great pain.
Your prayers are what got me through,
You have been faithful and true.
Again, I thank the Lord for you,
May you be blessed in all you do.
For those who have driven me everywhere,
And even given me your clothes to wear,
I praise the Lord whenever I can,
That you were all a part of God's great plan,
I thank you and give Him the glory,
When I tell this wonderful story.
For those who have prayed for me so faithfully,
Your thanks will go on eternally.
So as you read this poem, dear friends of mine,
May you see your names on each line.
I know I wouldn't be where I am today,
Your life has touched me in a special way.
So with that, I just want to say,

Thank you from the bottom of my heart,
Thank you for giving me a start.
My love to you, I do impart.
Please know I have tried to do the same.
And be a good friend in Jesus's name.
—Jean Bufton

This was written by my friend and incorporates all I have said in this chapter. Thanks, Julie!

F—Friends are unique gifts to each other.
R—Receive warmth and caring from one another.
I—Interested in the big and small things in life.
E—Encouraging when the going is tough.
N—No pretense—this is who and what I am.
D—Delight in honesty and transparency.
S—Shares joys, concerns, and sorrows.
H—Helpful, practical yet spiritual togetherness.
I—Inspire to live in freedom for God.
P—Pray for God's guidance for this special
Gift from God—my friend.
—Juliette Misar

Chapter 10

California, Here We Come!
(Lord, That Mountain Looks Pretty High
from This Valley We Are In)

All through January of 1985, we sought the Lord like never before. We were at another fork in the road, or a crossroad, if you will. We were at a time in our lives when we could move just about anywhere. We had always wanted to live in California, but really, we wanted the Lord's will. So again, we turned to His Word. Proverbs 16:1 reads, "We can make our plans, but the final outcome is in God's hands." God does have the best plan for us.

With great caution and much prayer, we made a trip to California to see if that was where God was leading us. After spending ten days there, I was offered a position in Beverly Hills. Doors were opened; God led. It was confirmed through many circumstances that we were to take a step of faith and move. It was one of the most difficult decisions we had ever made. We had to put our two feet in the water by faith and then God parted the sea.

We had very little money, but heaps of faith and trust. Bill had gone through much discouragement with the business and had to sell it at a time when the economy was down. At this time in his life, this was a big step to take.

HOPE FOR THE DAYS AHEAD

Again, we took refuge in the Word. I have marked in my Bible January 19, 1985 alongside of Zechariah 8:6. The Lord says, "This seems unbelievable to you—a remnant, small and discouraged as you are—but this is no great thing for Me. You can be sure that I will rescue you, My people, from the 'east and west.' I will bring them home again to live safely and they will be My people and I will be their good and loyal God." We actually felt the truth of God's promise as we claimed that verse for our lives. It did seem unbelievable. We *were* small, and Bill was somewhat discouraged. But look what the Lord was saying: "You can be sure that I *will* rescue you from the east and the west, and you will live safely. You will be my people and I will be your loyal God."

Again and again, I stand in amazement when I read the Word. Over and over, I claim His promises. I know these were written long ago, but I believe they are for us today, and I claim every one of them.

We felt like God was leading and preparing us for a new life and ministry in California. This was an awesome thought and responsibility, but one we felt the Lord was calling us to do. Now that we were stripped of anything that would hold us back like our business, home, or finances, we were free to step out in faith and go forth in peace. Again and again, we claimed the confirmation in Zechariah 3:10, "You will live in peace and prosperity and you will own a home of your own where you can invite your neighbors." We could not believe it! We did not even know if we wanted to own a home again because of the expense and responsibility. But the Lord said we would, we claimed it and left for California in February of 1985.

We call this our Valley experience and that is where we lived—in the San Fernando Valley. We found a condominium in Sepulveda. I was working in Beverly Hills at the time, so it was a convenient location, God opened the door for me to work as a personal assistant to actress Charlene Tilton. We were blessed to be friends and spiritual mentors to her and her family and still are to this day. God makes no mistakes where He leads us! Bill began to pursue employment, which was not as easy as he thought. To this day, we still stand in awe at how we made it financially.

I remember when we were getting ready to move. I did not know what furniture to bring, so I prayed that we would sell what we did not need and bring the rest. At the time, we had some beautiful antique wicker porch furniture, and it did not sell, so we brought it with us. Now we did not have a porch in California, and we had to store it in the garage, but the Lord knew we would need it in California in a different way. I was able to sell it one month to cover our rent payment. Thank You, Lord. You know what we need and how that need will be met. He has done it over and over, and I know He continues to meet the needs in our lives today.

We knew we needed Christian fellowship, so we were visiting a few churches in the area but had not found the right one. We remember when Jim Counihan, the evangelist who led Bill to the Lord, called one day and asked, "Have you found a good church yet? If not, I know of one you may like to visit. Bob Ricker is the pastor. He was my roommate at Bethel College in Minnesota. The church is called Faith Evangelical, and it is on the California State University at Northridge campus." CSUN was only ten minutes from us. Oh Lord, You *do provide*. We called Pastor Bob and told him we would be visiting the following Sunday.

I never will forget our first impression as we walked on that campus. We saw hundreds of people actually setting up a church (they had been doing this for ten years). From Sunday school classes to nurseries, from children's classes to adult classes, they would haul in coffee pots, plants, and playpens. They set up all of the sound, electrical equipment, and even the chairs for the auditorium where they met for church. They had a platform for the choir and a podium for the pastor. As Pastor Bob began to speak, we sensed a spirit of love, commitment, and the Lord in that congregation. As the choir sang, we could feel the joy. We looked around at all of these friendly, dedicated people and sensed a warm, comfortable, secure feeling; just what we needed.

Pastor Bob and his wife, Dee, had invited us to their house for lunch that day, and we met the couple who would become our first and dearest friends, Rodney and Margaret King. They immediately took us under their wing and ministered to us in a way we will never forget. We did not even know at the time just how much we needed it, but the Lord knew and provided us with these dear people. We were so touched by the love and graciousness of both the Rickers and the Kings, and the dedication and friendliness of the people at the church. Together, we felt that was where God wanted us to worship.

By that time, we were having a Valley experience with Bill still needing a job and the change of pace our lives had suddenly taken. Being away from our family for the first time was very difficult. The Lord knew we needed a church family, and they were there for us with open arms. Wherever God guides, He does provide. Yes, we had taken a giant step of faith, and He did part the sea. He did not say it would be easy, but He did say, "I *will* be with you."

He had not only been with us but sent people to befriend us. The Kings proceeded to invite us to their home the following Sunday evening to meet more people from the church. Hospitality truly is their spiritual gift. They opened their hearts and home to everyone. They have the unique ability to make everyone feel so welcome, comfortable, and right at home.

Each week, we would get together in someone's home and that was an opportunity for us to meet so many people. Rodney would introduce Bill to all of the businessmen in hopes of finding Bill a job. Before too long, that did happen. Just when Bill was at the end of himself and had exhausted all of his resources, God provided him with a contact, a Christian businessman from the church, Gene Hiebert. Gene introduced him to Bill Abbott who set up an interview with a large company in Sylmar. Praise God, Bill got the job. He started at Bendix Oceanic in July of 1985, six long months after we arrived in California.

I do not think we even knew at the time just how exhausted we were and how much we needed restoration and recuperation. What we really needed was a general refilling of our spirits and strength. We were burned out, in a sense. It definitely was a time of pruning, purging, and rebuilding for us. Our financial resources were gone, and we had to totally rely on God. Today, we can say our Valley experience was good for us, and we did finally see the flowers. Not on the mountaintops, but right there in the valley. There is a familiar saying: "bloom where you are planted." Well, we were planted in that Valley, and gradually, we did begin to bloom again. We were surrounded with all of these lovely, lovable people. Their lives were the flowers we saw, and their fragrance filled us with God's love. We were watered by the Word and nurtured by the message we heard.

We were cared for and put in the right place so we could grow, and grow we did. The Bible tells us in 1 Peter 5:10 that "after you have suffered for a little while, our God, who is full of kindness, will come and pick you up and put you firmly in place and make you stronger than ever." That is just what He did. It was good for us to be on the receiving end for a change. We had always given in time, talent, teaching, and tithe; and now we had to graciously receive those gifts from others. We found out it is as precious a gift to be able to receive as it is to give. And for the first time, we experienced what it meant for people to be in that position. It was a difficult time, but we do praise the Lord for the experience and what we learned through it.

Although we did not understand it completely at the time, we knew the Lord would use this time of testing to help us to, in turn, minister to others. How can we know what people are feeling if we have not experienced it ourselves? Believe me, this experience not only made us more sensitive, but also prepared us for our ministry today. Yes, again, Romans 8:28 is true: "All things do work together for good for those who love God and are called according to His purpose."

As we slowly continued to get our feet firmly in place, our spirits restored and our energy and enthusiasm reestablished, we began speaking and teaching again. It was good to be back on track. Not on top of the mountain by any means, but we could at least see it from where we were, and our vision became clearer as we grew closer to the Lord and each other. This was a trying time since we were accustomed to living close to our extended family. We gained a deeper sensitivity to our kids who had a long-distance love line going.

God had a pleasant surprise in that area too. By August of that year, our son-in-law, daughter, and first grandson, David, decided to move to California. Dave wanted to enroll in Logos Bible School and to pursue his career as a computer analyst in a sophisticated machine shop nearby that did work for the aerospace industry.

We began to look for a larger and safer place to live because they were going to stay with us for a while. As God would have it, He already had a place picked out.

One Sunday afternoon as we were looking for a larger condo, we saw one for sale and noticed the owner was having an open house. We liked the area. It was like a little quiet community in itself called Rockpointe in Chatsworth. We knew we could not buy anything, but we just wanted to see the size and all. When we walked in, we were so surprised to see the compact yet spacious four-bedroom condo, with two full baths. We really fell in love with it and knew it would be perfect for our two families. The owner was not there, but we left our number for her to call us in case she was interested in leasing it. She called that night, and there was instant rapport. I told her we were praying about a perfect place for our family, and she was thrilled to hear we were Christians and said she was praying for the right family to buy it. At that time, she had a contract with a realtor, but said she would call us if she could not sell it and wanted to lease it.

I did not hear from her for several weeks until one morning when I was having my devotions and the Lord impressed upon me to call her. When this thought came to me over and over, I thought, *Okay. It must be from you, Lord.* So I called, and when I told her who I was, she cried because she said she had just been praying that morning that I would call since she had lost our phone number.

We need to not only pray even for phone numbers, but be sensitive to the Lord's nudging through the Holy Spirit and be obedient. I have had this happen so many times and realize how important it is to follow through. What an answer to prayer for both of us! She could not sell the condo and wanted to lease it to us. We gave our notice and moved in the next month. The following month, our kids came to live with us. Once they got acclimated and established, they leased a condo nearby. As it turned out, after a year or so, we were able to buy the condo on a lease-purchase land contract deal that she set up. She was an attorney, and it was good for her and great for us. Again, we praise God for His provisions.

We lived there for two years and were very content. The real estate market had been in a slump during that time, and we really had no intention of selling or moving anywhere. We were regaining our equity at an affordable rate and were thankful for it. Well, as the roller coaster trend in California real estate goes, sure enough, it began to soar again. Lo and behold, we were sitting on a valuable piece of property with the potential for a lot of equity. In 1988, the going price for condos was at an all-time high. A real estate friend of ours told us that if we ever wanted to sell our condo, now was the time. It was also a good time to buy a home, she said, which would be a better investment. We really had not thought about it, but we prayed and said that if the Lord wanted us to sell it, we would. So we listed the condo and gave the realtor a one-month contract.

That very day when the realtor was putting the "for sale" sign in the yard, a lady who lived two doors down came over and said, "I want to buy your condo. I am renting one just like it and have been waiting for one to go up for sale." She came in and made us an offer, and within twenty minutes, it sold! We all stood in shock and amazement and said, "Yes, Lord, evidently, You did have this in mind for us."

We then began looking for a home. At that time, our son Jay was living with us, and Bill's mom was considering moving from Indiana to California to be with us. So we found the perfect home in Simi Valley with enough room for everyone to stay with even an extra room for guests and a nice yard. Bill and I remembered the verse the Lord gave us back in 1985 when we were leaving for California. It was Zechariah 3:10, "You will live in peace and prosperity and you will own a home of your own where you can invite your neighbors."

We again rejoiced and praised the Lord for His faithfulness because we were living in peace, and we were prospering. Because of His promises, we now had a home of our own again.

And yes, we did invite our friends and neighbors to come, and we did give God the glory. He had restored us in every area. We felt a little like Job and stood in humble awe and praise.

You could say we literally climbed Faith Mountain, as our church, which was Faith Church at the time, had purchased property on what they called Faith Mountain. Actually, it was the Rocky Peak area of Chatsworth between the San Fernando Valley and Simi Valley. We had moved from one valley to the other and had joined the church when it made its move to the mountain. It was so exciting for us to see how even our lives were to be a part of that move or climb. With great faith and courage, we climbed the mountain; and as we stood up there with the heavens as our ceiling and the Valley as the floor, we all prayed that this church—this body of believers—would make an impact for Christ in the many communities in the Valley below. We served at the church for four years. Bill served on the elder board and was a leader in our Sunday school class. Together, we led a twelve-week class for engaged couples called Fit to be Tied. We had the privilege of ministering to over two hundred couples, preparing them for marriage.

In 1986, our pastor, Bob Ricker, left and took a position as president of the Baptist General Conference in Illinois. In August of 1987, Dr. David Miller came as our pastor, and I began working in the church office as the receptionist. I loved my job and was excited about every area of ministry, especially ministering to women. Being at the front desk and receiving so many phone calls, I sensed the "heartbeat" of the needs of the church and the women. Many times, it would be a call for prayer or even some gentle words of counsel.

My heart was already touched in this area when Pastor Dave called me into his office and asked if I would consider coordinating something for the women in our church. I remember thinking what a tremendous task it would be. How could we meet the needs of so many women? I knew there was a great desire to study God's Word as we had several Bible studies already available. I also saw the Women's Missionary Circle meetings, which I was thankful for, but I knew too there were great needs in other areas.

Immediately, I went to the Lord in prayer and that is how Women's Ministries started in prayer. I searched the scriptures for an answer. On July 25, 1988 (I marked the date in my Bible), I found these verses in Isaiah 50:4–5: "The Lord God has given me His words of wisdom so that I may know what to say to all those weary ones (in need). Morning by morning, He awakens me and opens my understanding to His will. The Lord God had spoken to me and I listened." There was my answer. This was the Lord's ministry. He knew what the needs were. He would give me His words of wisdom and His understanding for the needs. He also knew that I needed other women who were gifted in areas to join with me in this ministry and serve the women in our church. I prayed for these Godly women, and one-by-one, the Lord brought them together. Each one gifted in a different area, and together, they completed the first Women's Ministries team. They were Claudia Davis, Gayle Martz, Bev Pollock, Loree Goens, Karen Bollier, and Tedi Kinney. Each one was a coordinator of these specific areas: Women in Touch, Women Aware, Women in the Word, Women at Home, Women in Service, and Women in Prayer.

My thought was to have representation from every age group, linking all of the women together. We needed one more representative from the Forever Young group (one with white hair!).

The one area that was not represented was the area I thought was the most important as it would serve as the foundation for all the rest, and that was the area of prayer. The Lord knew what we needed and had already prepared the way.

CALIFORNIA, HERE WE COME!

I can still remember the day I was at the desk and a call came in. It was Tedi Kinney. She shared her concern with me regarding the area of prayer and wanted to see if we could start a prayer chain for the church. I praised the Lord on the spot, and as we continued our conversation, we both sensed we had the same burden and desire to have women who pray as part of our team. I asked her to serve on our team and head up the Women in Prayer committee. Tedi prayerfully considered this enormous responsibility. When she said yes, our team was complete (she even had white hair!).

In August 1988, we met to pray. At that time, the task seemed monumental, but we knew it was God's ministry, and He had called us to serve. With that, we claimed 1 Chronicles 28:20: "Be strong and courageous—get to work! Don't be frightened by the size of the task, for the Lord my God is with you. He will not forsake you. He will see to it that everything is finished correctly."

With that, we proceeded in His strength and confidence. Our desire and purpose was to provide opportunities for women to be established in the Word, equipped for ministry, and encouraged to reach out. We stood in awe as God directed us and blessed us in so many ways. We saw lives being changed and needs being met, and the ministry grew.

We each felt a need to have an assistant, so we expanded our team to include Bev Cargo, Carol Flaig, Lynn Badgett, Esther Kitchen, Nita Mitchell, Candy Wood, Lisa Bollier, Geri Andrews, and Sharon Ahlstrom. Each one was responsible for a specific area of ministry, reaching out still farther to the needs of the women in the areas of encouragement, Women Who Care (hospitality, calling new women, singles, aerobics, discipleship), Sisters of Support, and Forever Young (a fifty-five-plus singles group). Others who served so faithfully were Gem Fadling, Marty Kemp, Viviaette O'Brien, Donna Wern, Jan Brady,

Carolyn Yeargain, Robin Kosmaia, Carol Reid, Carol Zurcher, Laurie Pearson, Carolyn Myers, Kathy Likes, Linda Thompson, Elsie Zimmerman, Karen Patterson, Arlene O'Grady, Karen Butler, Aldeen Clemmons, Rosanna McElveen, and Doris Macomb.

I was so thankful for each one who stood with me, prayed for me, and served so faithfully. There were so many others who responded in *many areas* of service. I would have to write another book in order to include their names, but they know the Lord knows of their faithfulness and how together, we did God's work at The Church at Rocky Peak for His glory. This was another verse the Lord gave us and it says it all: "May He grant you your heart's desire and fulfill all your plans. May there be shouts of joy when we hear the news of your victory, flags flying with praise to God for all that He has done for you. May He answer all of your prayers" (Ps. 20:4–5). And that He did! We praise Him for it. It was a glorious time, and we loved every minute of it.

I remember when the Lord first put the thought in my mind of the possibility of leaving the Director of Women's Ministries position I loved so much. It was really a year before we even had any idea that we would be moving, but God has a way of preparing our spirits first. As I began to pray, He put a name in my heart, and I prayed and believed and was excited about who the Lord chose to replace me in my position. I was in complete agreement. I could not say anything for a while because the thought was like a mustard seed and needed to be bathed in prayer. This was before we had any intention of even thinking about moving anywhere.

At the appropriate time, I approached my dear friend, Carolyn Yeargain, about what the Lord had put on my heart.

Carolyn looked at me wide-eyed and teary, and said, "Oh, Jean. You're not thinking about leaving, are you? Don't go!"

CALIFORNIA, HERE WE COME!

I smiled and said, "I don't know what the Lord is doing, but I need you to pray with me." Carolyn is one of those great ladies with deep spiritual insight and a powerful prayer warrior. She knew instinctively what I was going to say even before I said it. In fact, we were so in tune, we could almost finish each other's sentences, or didn't even have to. We just *knew*. It was like Holy Spirit-inspired, and we were wired together spiritually. Carolyn had all of the gifts and qualities to be the director of Women's Ministries. In fact, she also had the added talent of being a teacher for over thirty years. She had taught our women's Bible study, a good listener, had discernment, and was a good counselor. Her greatest quality is she loved the Lord with all of her heart and loved to serve His people. In fact, she and her husband, Larry, had been serving the Lord as a couple for thirty-some years in various ministries at the churches where they were members, the most recent being leaders in one of the adult Sunday school classes at our church. Larry also served on the elder board with Bill, and together we spent many moments in prayer.

We would meet for what we would call our PP&P night which was Prayer, Praise, and Popcorn time. Yes, we praise the Lord for friends like the Yeargains. As we prayed together for our future and families, finances, and much more, we could see God's hand in both of our lives in the months to come. As our future plans unfolded and the possibility of us moving was becoming a reality, I knew more than ever in my heart that Carolyn was the one to take over my position. God had not confirmed that in Carolyn's heart yet, so we continued to pray.

I remember one day when I was talking to our pastor about it, and he said, "I have a thought of who could take over your position, Jean."

I said, "Yes? So do I."

I asked him to share his thoughts first and he said, "Carolyn Yeargain."

I smiled and rejoiced in my spirit as I felt that was another confirmation. I shared my praise with Carolyn, but still, she did not feel free to make the commitment at that time. What was so cute was that she kept saying, "Don't go!" But as the weeks and months went by, it definitely looked like, yes, in fact, we *were* going to *go!*

I remember being in a staff meeting during our time of prayer. I had shared the fact of our likely move and asked them to be praying for the decision for my position replacement. As we went around the room and prayed, Mike Millett, our junior high pastor, prayed something like this: "Lord, we do pray for the one You have chosen for this position. And Lord, not that You would have her fill Jean's shoes, but Lord, that You would design her own." Oh, how I rejoiced in that prophetic prayer. I quickly ran to the phone, called Carolyn, and relayed that message to her. I assured her she would have her own "designer shoes" to wear. We laughed and cried, and prayed some more.

Then one day soon after, Carolyn called me and said, "Jean, the Lord has confirmed to me from His Word what my answer will be. He says in Ephesians 3:20, "Now glory be to God who by *His* mighty power at work in us is able to do far more than we would ever dare to ask or dream of—infinitely beyond our highest prayers, desires, thoughts or hopes." Yes, we both knew it was the Lord's power in us that we all needed and depended upon and trusted in. With that, Carolyn said yes!

This is a good example for all of us to learn. When we are asked to serve in any way, we need to first commit it to the Lord in prayer, release any pre-conceived thoughts and ideas, and wait until it is real clear from the Lord what you should do. This is so important so that we do not say yes for the wrong reasons and be doing something in the ministry with which we are

CALIFORNIA, HERE WE COME!

not comfortable. Carolyn was cautious and rightly so. When she got the confirmation from His Word, then she was confident with her decision and made the commitment. We both knew this was God's perfect plan for us, and God continued to bless the Women's Ministries under Carolyn's very competent direction at The Church at Rocky Peak.

When I left, I wrote these thoughts in a poem for all the ladies with whom I served on the Women's Ministries team:

> Ladies, this is a time when I hardly know what to say,
> But I'm coming to you on this day,
> With tremendous love and care from my heart,
> And with that I would like to start.
>
> My tribute is to each one of you,
> You have made my job so easy to do.
> For the endless hours you put in,
> I hardly know where to begin.
> I want to thank each of you,
> For the countless things you so lovingly do.
> After the Lord, I would get the glory,
> But everyone knows that's not my story.
> God sent each one of you with a special gift,
> Knowing that I would need a lift.
> You surrounded me with love and prayer,
> I always felt your constant care.
> When I couldn't count, spell or say "No!"
> You always smiled and let me go.
> You took on the extra responsibility and,
> Let me be my "Sanguine Me,"
> As I carried on God's ministry.

And now the Lord has opened another door,
A new opportunity to serve Him more.
He is allowing me a time in my life,
Where I will begin to write.
I know in my heart this is long overdue,
The words I have to say will be sincere and true.
I will tell what the Lord has meant to me,
As the book comes together, you will see,
What your friendship has meant to me.
I know I couldn't have done this without you,
These are my thoughts—honest and true!

Now I go with great joy and peace,
Because even though *my* work here will cease,
The ministry *will* continue on,
With your new director, Carolyn Yeargain.
She *is* God's answer to my prayer.
Please surround her with your love and care.
I truly believe this will be,
The *best* year *ever* for Women's Ministry.

I remain joyfully,
In Jesus's love and care,
With you in my heart and constant prayer.
—Jean
Romans 8:28

Those years at Faith Church on Faith Mountain were some of the greatest years of our lives. Yes, some of the toughest, but oh, what lessons we learned and have been able to share as a result. We really believe our Valley experiences are good for us.

We really need them to keep us close to the Lord and trust Him in our times of trials.

In 1990, the church's name was changed to The Church at Rocky Peak, and Bill and I continued to serve the Lord there in various ministries. People from back in Indiana or Illinois would ask us, "How do you like California, with all of the crime, characters, earthquakes, fast pace, and unfriendly people?" We would answer, "We love it because we know this is where God wants us to be at this time." We believe in that simple and much-used phrase, "bloom where you are planted." Of course, Paul says it much better: "Be content in whatever 'state' you're in," even if it is the "state" of California. We can be secure when the Lord is our foundation. We found the people to be very friendly. Crime is bad everywhere, not just in the Golden State. The earthquakes were a bit shaky, but tornadoes and hurricanes are scary too. If you are going through uncertain times right now and are facing unfamiliar decisions, if your ground is shaky and you have been in the valley so long you can't even begin to see the mountaintop, may I encourage you to trust the Lord and pray. Let go and let God lead you. Don't ask why, but ask, "What do You want me to learn, Lord, from this experience?"

If you are not already in a church or small support group, please seek one out. You need the caring, loving support of other Christians who can help and encourage you. We all need someone to talk to, fellowship with, grow closer to the Lord with, and to study God's Word with. We *do* need people like Jesus with arms to hug us and hearts to help us. Proverbs 3:5–6 says, "Trust the Lord. He *will* direct your path." He will direct you to the right church, person, and place to get help.

Yes, there is *Hope for the Days Ahead* even if you are in a valley right now. Remember that to get from one mountain top to another, you have to go through the valley.

Chapter 11

Lord, Can You Change the Dial on This Time of Trial?

See if you can relate to this statement: "The hardest area of my life was to *trust*. How do you *trust* when every time you have trusted, you were hurt? If only someone could help me in this area." This was the desperate cry of a dear friend of mine. She has given me permission to use her story in hopes that it will help someone who is hurting like she was.

I'll never forget the night I met my friend, Karen. It was at a church meeting. I was sitting alone and saw this attractive gal come in. I remember thinking, *Now here's someone who has it all together—blond hair, sparkling eyes, beautiful smile, well dressed, as cute as can be.* Little did I know what she was feeling when she came in. Yes, her outward appearance was "all together," and she did love the Lord, but she was feeling very insecure that night walking in alone. She said she looked around the room, hoping to find someone she could sit next to. When she spotted me alone, she came over and asked if the seat next to me was taken.

I said, "Oh no. Please sit here." It was an instant rapport, and of course, pre-planned by God. We giggled and chatted, and when we realized we had the same outgoing personalities, we both signed up to be hostesses for our Easter Sunday celebration.

After the meeting that night, Karen and I sat in my car and talked for a long time. She felt like she could trust me and felt comfortable sharing what she was going through at the time. I remember seeing the tears well up and fill those sparkling eyes of hers. That radiant smile began to tremble as she spoke. I thought, *How many people do we see only from the outside and do not know how much they are hurting on the inside? We need to take time to listen.*

As I listened to her that night, Karen shared about her broken heart and broken home. She desperately needed help and hope. As we prayed together that night, it was the beginning of a very special friendship and prayer partnership. God knows what He is doing when He brings people together as friends because each with their different gifts, they do complement each other, as was in this case with Karen and me.

When I took on the responsibility of Director of Women's Ministries at our church, I asked Karen to be my assistant. She was a great help. Karen was gifted in many areas, and this gave her a sense of self-worth. She loved serving the Lord in this way. It was also a way we could spend time in the Word and in prayer as she went through this very difficult time in her life. God does bring people together so we can help one another, learn from one another, and of course, pray for each other.

As the years went by, each one became more difficult than the last for Karen. She wanted to make the marriage work, but it seemed hopelessly over.

After much counsel and prayer, when the decision was made, she thought it was the end for her. Karen explains the first three months this way:

> I went through the motions of living, but life was a blur. Had it not been for some very special friends that God placed in my life, I never would have made it. Carol, Carolyn, and Jean stood by me, prayed with me, allowed me to talk, cry, and even be angry. God was taking me along a path I did not want to go, but He was very gently and very patiently leading me to a better place. I wish I could say I was going along with God willingly, but I wasn't. I screamed at God and was very angry at Him. I questioned Him constantly and, even though I never said it, I even thought I hated Him for what He was allowing in my life. If He really loved me, He would never have allowed so much to happen to me. The pain was more than I could bear. But as usual, I was wrong. He did love me and cared for me, and was working out His perfect plan for my life.
>
> During the time of going through my divorce, along with the constant support of my friends, I also went to a Christian counselor. He was able to help me work through a lot of areas of my past. On top of dealing with my divorce—which was devastating enough—I found out I was molested as a child. This pain was so great I could hardly bear it. The more I discovered, the more

desperate I became. I knew I had to make a choice right then and there: was I going to dig deeper, or recognize it for what it was—a very tragic circumstance that I had no control over? I chose at that moment to put my life under God's control and to allow Him to work through the restoration I needed to heal my hurts. This was the hardest area of my life to trust in. There are three things that should not be broken: trusts, hearts, and promises. Unfortunately, these can cause us to lose our *trust* in God, others, and even in ourselves at times. There is a song that says, "Only trust Him, only trust Him. He will see you through." This is true but very hard to do.

One afternoon, when Karen was at her lowest point, I called someone she trusted who had ministered to her years ago. Allegra Harrah and her husband, Cal, lived in Redlands, close to us. When I spoke with them and shared the urgency of the situation, they responded in this way: "We will be there as soon as possible."

They arrived that afternoon, and I watched in silent prayer as this dear, godly couple ministered to her with patience, kindness, and much wisdom. They shared many truths, but one thing Allegra said was so profound that my friend Karen responded immediately to it.

Allegra told Karen, "You are having trouble releasing this area of trust to the Lord. So I want you to open both of your hands with your palms up and give God permission to take it from you."

Karen replied, "You are right. I cannot give it to God, but I will give Him permission to take it from me."

I am sure many of you can relate to that. It is so hard to let go and trust God. As unusual as it sounds, sometimes when the pain is so great, it is actually almost like a protection of the past. It is a false one, but nonetheless, it does protect a person from dealing with the pain. It is so complicated but so real in the lives of many.

We do have to take the first step of faith in trusting Him. That evening, Karen made her choice. She chose to ask God to take her lack of faith and lack of trust from her. She said, "I gave and He took, and at that moment, I began a new freedom. The victory came, but *not* overnight—it was a slow process." Too often, we want an instant cure for our pain. It sometimes happens that way, but not very often. There is a process to healing this intense pain.

Karen went on to say:

> God was so patient with me as I went through this time. All through those months, I was not able to read anything but the Psalms. But oh, how they helped me. I learned that He is a trustworthy God—trustworthy and true. I know now that this area of my life was not what God would have chosen for me, but He did take what Satan meant for evil and use it for good!
>
> God also used people to pray for me and with me during this crucial time. They encouraged me, stood by me, and just *loved* me unconditionally. They always directed me back to my only source of *hope*—Jesus. Over and over, I heard and read that Jesus really did love me, and He does care about every little detail of my life. I can say this with assurance

because in October of 1990, I wrote a list of all the desires of my heart; and in February of 1991, He answered every single one.

During Karen's healing and restoration *process*, I remember many times of counseling in my office. She would be crying so hard from the depths of her heart that the tears would literally drop out of her eyes onto her lap. She would say, "Jean, I am so lonely. I see couples everywhere being together and doing things together. I feel so out of place. I feel like I am the third or fifth wheel. No one makes me feel that way—it's just me. I need someone to belong to!"

How often do we hear this? Loneliness has to be the most devastating, painful thing to go through. It is so important to feel a part of, or belong to someone. The loneliness of divorce in some ways is almost harder than the death of a loved one.

Karen went on to say, "All my life, all I have ever wanted was to have a Christian home. I love being a wife and mother. I see couples going to church and Bible studies and ministering together, going on weekend retreats and vacations, having fun socially—I want to do all that so badly. Do you think God knows how desperately I desire that, Jean?"

I would say, "Yes. He knows your needs and understands your desperation, and He will give you the desires of your heart in His time. I do not know when that will be, but I know He is trustworthy and true to His promises." I reminded Karen of the promise He gave her in Habakkuk 1:5: "I am going to do something in your life that you will have to see to believe." And Habakkuk 2:3 says, "But please be *patient*. It won't be overdue one single day."

I also reminded her of something that I think is so significant for all of us to remember: we all need to come to a place in our lives where Jesus is all we need. Yes, even before our husband, children, parents, family, or friends. Too often, we look to them to meet our needs, and they cannot. I told her she needed to yield to Him in this area. Let go and let God have control. "Remember," I told her, "the choice is yours."

Again, she opened her hands and asked God to take it and fill her with Himself and His peace. Not too long after, God answered Karen's prayers and gave her the desires of her heart. Karen's story is a testimony of God's faithfulness and perfect plan for all of our lives. "If we *trust* with all of our hearts, He will direct our paths."

We know this: God *is* sovereign, and we know His plans are best for us. We do not always understand them at the time, but as we see them unfold, we can say, "Yes. Your will be done."

As Karen was going through these very difficult days, another friend of ours was going through a difficult time also. Renny Bollier, who was a dear Christian brother in our church, was going through the heartache of losing his wife to cancer. We as a church body were praying for him and continued as he went through his time of grief, pain, and healing. It is interesting to note that we were all praying for him even before the Lord put a thought in our minds about the possibility of bringing him and Karen together. But as the months went on, several of us had the thought but kept it in our prayers only.

One day, Karen came to me and shared the list of qualities she desired for a godly man and Christian husband. I could hardly believe what I was hearing as they fit Renny to a *T*. This was unbelievable. Then she went on to say, "Jean, the Lord has been speaking to me about a specific person."

I said, "Oh? Who might that be?" My heart was pounding in excitement. *Could it be, Lord?* I thought to myself.

As she said Renny's name, her face lit up, and her eyes glistened as she shared from her heart what the Lord was confirming in her spirit. Karen was overjoyed when I shared my thoughts with her about Renny and told her I had been praying about that for months, so were our other two closest friends, Carol and Carolyn. We all had the same confirmation from the Lord and had been bathing it in prayer.

"In His time, in His time. He makes all things beautiful in His time." So go the lyrics to a beautiful Christian song. It certainly applies to the special timing in this couple's lives.

Karen and Renny had a wonderful and unusual courtship. They actually began dating and courting on the telephone. They would talk on the phone for hours, just sharing and getting to know one another. Believe it or not, they were building a foundation of love and respect in their conversations on the phone. We laughingly said, "Only a sanguine like Karen can fall in love over the telephone," and fall in love they did. They courted, dated, and were married in August of 1991. Renny brought four children and a daughter-in-law; Karen had two boys and a daughter-in-law. Their families blended beautifully.

This was another blessing from the Lord. Another verse the Lord gave Karen was this one, and she claimed it! "These plans I have for you are for good," says the Lord in Jeremiah 29:11. Yes, we all feel this marriage was definitely part of God's plan for them. They both had experienced great pain and great loss. They had their time of grieving and healing. They both had found their security in the Lord and now He had brought them together.

The desire of their hearts was to serve the Lord as a couple. They were sponsors for our college group at church and then they began team-teaching the engaged couples' class with us. Little did we know at the time that God was preparing Karen and Renny to take over our class the following year when we left. God has the best plan for us and in *His* time, prepares us for it.

HOPE FOR THE DAYS AHEAD

I quote Karen, "The key is prayer. Even when I could not pray, there was someone praying for me. I know that is the only reason I have victory today. Pray, pray, pray! It works! I can say without a doubt that Jesus does care. He does love me, and He will do for you what He has done for me."

Perhaps you are in a similar situation and can relate to all or some of what I shared about what happened to this couple. I know their prayer would be as mine was; that it will give you hope and encouragement, and bring into focus God's faithfulness. I *trust* this story and testimony will be an encouragement to anyone who is single, gone through the loss of a spouse, or who has gone through a divorce. To God be the glory!

Trust can begin early in life. It does not matter how old you may be, this foundation of faith and trust is invaluable; start while your children are young. Their minds are so open and imaginative especially in the six-ish years. Also, a word to you grandparents: you can be very instrumental in your grandchildren's lives. We have had some great experiences with our grandchildren, but one stands out in my mind. This was written by Bill as it happened that memorable Memorial Day in 1991:

> Back in May of 1991, I was listening to *Focus on the Family* with my favorite talk show host, Dr. James Dobson. On this particular morning, he was interviewing a couple by the name of Mr. and Mrs. Doug Kingsrider who were discussing their ministry to children. Being a sports fan, I recognized Doug's name immediately as he was a former member of the Minnesota Vikings football team. He and his wife were introducing "GT and the Halo Express," a cassette ministry of singing scrip-

ture verses which children could easily learn. Naturally, I went out and bought them for my grandchildren.

On that particular day, Dr. Dobson and his guests were discussing how children and adults have fear in their lives. They went on to explain Psalm 56:3, "When I am afraid, I will trust in God!"

When my grandsons David and Jonathan showed up the next Friday evening, I asked them what they would like to do. "Oh," they exclaimed, "let's get a video!" This is where compromise came in. There had to be an exchange, and I then explained in detail the new game plan to them. If they would learn a scripture verse, we would go get a video. What verse do you think I introduced to them? Yes, Psalm 56:3. They were both eager to hear and learn this verse. Little did I know how this verse would affect my life in the next few weeks!

At the end of May, our son-in-law's grandmother passed away in Indiana, so he and our daughter traveled back East for five days. Naturally, Jean and I watched the grandchildren during that time. On Memorial Day, as I have many times, I took David and Jonathan to the horse rides and then to eat at their favorite place—McDonald's. Then we went to a local park.

As I sat watching them play for some time, I looked up and saw Jonathan going up the silo-type slide (a round tube that you climb inside and then come to the top and slide down). On this last climb, I could hear a loud crunch followed by a series of clunks. As I looked down on the final thud, I saw Jonathan lying in a limp, listless position with blood spurting from his eye area. As I picked him up, I was afraid, thinking all sorts of negative thoughts. I thought he had been knocked unconscious. As I put a t-shirt over this fountain of blood, I began to pray. *Oh Lord, please don't let him be hurt too badly.* I could not drive and hold him as I knew we had to get to the hospital. God is so good and gracious. There was another man with his two children, and he immediately came to my aide and said, "Let's go to the hospital at once."

After what seemed like hours but was only five to ten minutes, we arrived at the hospital. During this period of fear, I asked Jonathan on the way if he was okay. I told him, "I love you, Jesus loves you, David is here, and he loves you. Are you all right?" Because you see, he cried not a tear during this entire episode, and I remember his muffled reply through the sea of red blood on the shirt that I had put over his face. It was with a breath of reply that I rejoiced.

He simply said, "When I am afraid, I will trust in God"—the verse he had just learned.

When we went into the emergency room at the hospital, they immediately ushered me into a room, and at that point began all the questions. Very honestly, I could hardly remember addresses, telephone numbers, names, etc. I simply but emphatically stated, "Let's go!"

First, a nurse came in and started to clean his face. Jonathan flinched, but never cried. I prayed, cried, and called out to the Lord! The nurse said that I could bring David in to see his brother. David got up on a stool, leaned over, and laid his hand on his brother's chest and began to pray out loud that God would heal his brother's wound. David ended by saying, "You know that I love you very much." I must confess, by this time, tears were streaming down my face.

David went back to the waiting room and the on-duty doctor, along with three nurses, came into the room. My first thought was, why three nurses? I soon found out! The doctor told me to hold Jonathan's legs down and the three nurses were to hold his head and arms still. The doctor explained that he would probably buck like a horse once he started. They washed his head with Betadine soap that went everywhere. As they cleaned him, for the first time, I could see where the cut was—just above his right eye, about half an inch away from the eye. They then put this hood over his head with a slot in it, and the doctor told us, "Really hold him. I am going to shoot Novocain in the area," which he did about five or six times, and Jonathan did not move or cry. As I held his legs, I noticed they were in a state of relaxation. The doctor started the stitching process. I asked the nurses to let Jonathan go, and they did.

The doctor explained to me that he had ripped the muscle and he had to do the inside work, which he did with fifteen to eighteen stitches, along with twelve stitches on the outside. He asked Jonathan, "Son, are you all right?"

Jonathan's answer was, "When I am afraid, I will trust in God."

The doctor looked at me, smiled, and said, "Then I know you are going to be okay!"

It took an excruciating period of thirty to forty minutes to finish, and as the doctor was about done, I could hear Jonathan give a big sigh; and I honestly thought he had fallen asleep. I told the doctor what I thought—he *was* asleep! As the hood was removed, Jonathan sat upright on the table and profoundly stated, "Let's go home!" and once more he told a happy doctor and a relieved Grandpa, "When I am afraid, I will trust in God."

I picked him up, hugged him, and carried him out.

Yes, we would all like to turn down the thermostat dial in our time of trial, but God knows the temperature we need. He says in 1 Peter 1:7, "These trials are only to test your faith to see whether it is strong and pure. It is being tested as fire tests gold and purifies it; if it remains strong after going through the fire, it will bring much praise and glory and honor on the day of His return."

We do need to remain strong—we need to *totally trust God* with our family, our future, and our finances. Hopefully, you will be able to claim the words to this song now: "Trust Him, only trust Him. He will see you through."

In closing, as we again look at the word *TRUST*, perhaps this acrostic will help you:

> *T—Turn* your unknown future over to an all-knowing God.
> *R—Relinquish* the control of your life completely to the Lord
> *U—Unlock* the pain from the past and receive healing for your hurts.
> *S—Surrender* every area of your life to the Lord.
> *T—Take* your hands off the situation. Open them and ask God to take whatever it is you are holding on to away.

You cannot do any of this on your own strength, but you can with help—His—and that of a good Christian counselor. The choice is yours. Make a commitment today to trust Christ with your life.

Chapter 12

Let's Synchronize Our Watches, Lord

In 1991 (it seems like our life runs in a seven-year cycle), we were coming into our seventh year in California, and we were loving it! Bill had just invested in a small machine shop and was back in business again. This was something he had always wanted to do again. I was happily working at our church as the director of Women's Ministries. We both were active in other ministries as well, teaching classes called Fit to be Tied for engaged couples and Prime Time for the singles group. Bill also led a Bible study in our home.

We were as busy and as happy as we could be—all settled into this wonderful ministry. Uh-oh. You know what happens when you get too settled and too comfortable and here it was again, just like in Illinois, that seventh year coming up. It began to look like we were being prepared for a new adventure.

By Christmas of that year, things began to get a little shaky in the business world. It wasn't a literal earthquake, but rather we were experiencing aftershocks from the economic earthquake. Bill looked ahead and saw what was happening to the aerospace industry, especially small business. We began to pray and seek God's will and direction.

From Christmas through March, we faced a lot of uncertainties. With Operation Desert Storm and all that was going on in the world, our concerns seemed so small in comparison, but we continued to pray for answers for all concerned. Then, out of the blue (heaven), someone offered to buy our business. We were not looking to sell, but it was a *solid* cash offer. We were a little taken aback, so we quickly called our attorney and accountant for advice and counsel.

Knowing what the economy was like and projecting the future of the aerospace industry, they advised us to seriously consider this offer. In fact, we all felt like it was definitely from God, as not too many people come to your door these days with cash, wanting to buy your business. Negotiations began, and by July, they were finalized at just the right time. Bill sought employment in California during that summer, but with all of the aerospace layoffs and companies moving out of state, the jobs were few and far between.

We had made plans for later that summer to visit our son Bill and his family who were living in Atlanta at the time. Bill thought he could use this time to get a feel for what the economy was like and the possibility of a job opportunity there. We really did not have any definite plans, and as always, we were trusting in the Lord to "show us the path where we should go." That week in Atlanta was *very* interesting; we know in hindsight that God had it all planned. When we arrived, our dear, longtime friends, Don and Rita Bruno, greeted us warmly and were excited about the possibility of us moving there. It was remote at the time, but again, we were seeking the Lord's will.

While we were there, we had the opportunity to meet Tom Grady who was a friend of a real-estate agent that Rita knew. She said that we would probably have a lot in common, and she was right—we did. We called him that week, and he was available to meet with us for lunch that Wednesday. That meeting was the beginning of another life-changing experience for us.

Tom was the president of Grace Fellowship International in Atlanta. It is a non-profit, non-denominational organization created for the purpose of helping to equip the members of the body of Christ to effectively communicate the message of the cross, knowing Christ as Savior, Lord, and Life based on Galatians 2:20. This is accomplished through a two-fold approach—counseling and counselor training. We were excited to hear about this ministry and were blessed to hear that they never turn any client away even if they cannot afford counseling. We were also very interested in hearing more about the message. We have always felt that knowing your identity in Christ is the key to a victorious Christian life. Tom invited us to one of their Exchanged Life Conferences when we came back, and we looked forward to that!

We left feeling like this was the beginning of a very special friendship and that somehow, our lives would never be the same, and they haven't been since. The story that follows is a perfect example of God's faithfulness, sovereignty, and plan for all of our lives. God knows what we need, and He provides it through His Word, the people we meet, and the places we go. "Before we were born, our lives were planned" (Ps. 139).

In September, I went to Illinois to be with my father when he had knee surgery, so Bill went back to Atlanta to pursue looking for employment at Lockheed. While he was there, two very interesting things happened: he had an interview at Lockheed, and he attended an Exchanged Life Conference. It just so happened that Tom was giving one that very week, and Bill was there (again, I couldn't have planned it better). God *was* in control, and His timing was perfect! That conference was life changing for Bill, and he wrote in his own words what transpired:

> In September of 1991, I was introduced to some spiritual truths in a three-day Exchanged Life Conference. God showed me the reality of Romans 5:8, Colossians 2:3, and Galatians 2:20. "I have been crucified with Christ and it is no longer I who live, but Christ who lives in me and the life which I now live in the flesh, I live by faith in the Son of God Who loved me and gave Himself up for me."
>
> For the first time in my life, I knew that God had totally accepted me, not based on my performance, but based on what Christ has accomplished on the cross. In all humility, I experienced complete brokenness for the first time in my life. I had found freedom and victory at the cross. I was so liberated I wanted everyone to know these truths and experience the death, burial, resurrection, and ascension with Christ as I had.

Bill called me from Atlanta, and I could not believe my ears. It wasn't only the job prospect or the area he was excited about, but it was the truths he heard in the Exchanged Life message. Again, the events that followed were incredible. Bill came back and began to teach what he had learned. The transformation in his own life was proof enough that it worked and was real.

In November, we both went back to Atlanta. I was able to attend an Exchanged Life Conference, and Bill had another good interview at Lockheed. I remember praying while he was interviewing, "Lord, please close the doors if this is not from You and open the doors if it is." The interview went great, and the doors were definitely open *with* a possible job opening by January. We came home and put our house on the market. This was a *very, very* tough and unusual time in California. The real-estate market was very weak, homes were not selling, and those that were being bought were being drastically reduced. But we knew from past experiences that the Lord was our realtor, and if He wanted our house to sell, it would be sold at just the right time. Again, we trusted the Lord and continued to serve Him.

Bill even added another ministry to his already busy schedule. While visiting a church in Marietta, GA we noticed they had a ministry for unemployed men. Bill was somewhat unemployed at the time, and there were so many men in our church who were too. So he started a support group for unemployed men. This gave them hope for the difficult days ahead. I know this is not the "norm" for men, but this was a great source of encouragement for them. They met, shared, and prayed. Through many helpful resources, they were able to hang in there while pursuing other employment. This is just another confirmation that God can and does use every circumstance we go through for good.

We did get through the holidays, and by January, it looked like the final interview and confirmation on Bill's job at Lockheed would be finalized by February. Bill was once more making plans to go to Marietta when Tom Grady called and said, "Bill, while you are here, I'd like you to attend a three-day retreat for men called Tres Dias. In fact, there has been a cancellation and I can get you in." There are those plans again. We honestly did not know at the time just how intense this preparation and plan was.

But believe me, it was! Usually, it's the women who enjoy and receive so much from a retreat and come back spiritually high and blessed from the inside out. Well, let me tell you, Bill said attending a Tres Dias weekend was like sitting at the feet of Jesus.

Truly, we have attended many seminars and retreats, but this weekend had the most *personal*, powerful impact of any. We recommend it for every man and woman, married or single, and there are also conferences for teenagers. We see now how God was preparing Bill for the days ahead, and me also for that matter, because I was able to attend the following weekend. I experienced the same impact of God's love through His Word and His people that Bill had. Yes, this was one of the spiritual highlights of our lives, the closest thing to heaven on earth.

While I was at the weekend retreat, an interesting thing happened. On Friday morning, Bill called the man he had been in contact with at Lockheed to arrange for his final interview. Much to his surprise and amazement, Bill listened intently to his reply. He had just come from a manager's meeting that morning, and a decision was made to freeze all applications and jobs for the time being. Needless to say, Bill was a little taken aback because this job description was written based upon his resume. But he thought, *My life is in Your hands, God. You know all about this.*

Bill had a pre-arranged breakfast meeting with Tom that morning. When they met, Tom said, "Bill, do you really want to go to work at Lockheed? I feel you should be in full-time ministry. I'd like to extend a call to you to consider the requirements and the preparation of coming on full time staff with us at Grace Fellowship. Begin to prayerfully consider this, and let me know God's answer as soon as possible."

Needless to say, Bill was totally overwhelmed. Not only had he always wanted to do this, but God's timing on the provision for it was unbelievable.

Bill left the meeting that morning knowing he needed to be alone with God. He drove to the country, prayed, and asked God to confirm to him what he should do. As in Proverbs 3:5–6, he was trusting in the Lord with all his heart, and he didn't lean on his own understanding because he didn't understand all of this completely. In all of his ways, he did acknowledge Him and was trusting Him to direct his path.

He arrived that day back at our friend's home—the Brunos—and shared what had just happened. Through their conversation, it was confirmed that this definitely was God's plan for him, and they would pray and support Bill as he prepared for this new ministry. They also opened their home for him to stay during the eight-week internship.

I was at the Tres Dias weekend at this time; but I have to say, when I learned about this, I was not surprised. We have always thought that someday, we would be in full-time ministry. This has been our dream and desire for many years. We felt like all that we went through was preparation for this time and plan of God's. Even those past six months, we see it very clearly now how God used even Lockheed as a part of His plan. If Bill did not feel he had a prospective job, he would not have made all those trips to Georgia; and if he had not made those trips, he would not have been able to attend the seminars or the Tres Dias weekend.

Do you see how God does have our days planned and how He does work all things together for our good? I know I have repeated this many times throughout this book, but it is true and a testimony to God's sovereignty and faithfulness. I love it when His plan comes together in His time. We need to be sensitive to His leading and submissive to His will.

Well, what was the next step for us for our new adventure? We both met with Tom for some counsel and direction. He gave us good advice and several options. He said we needed to first pray and seek God's positive confirmation, answer, and will for our lives if we felt like this was the way He was leading. Bill would have to attend a five-day workshop and then apply for an eight-week internship. Tom said that during that time, Bill would know if this was what God wanted him to do and where that would be. We felt at that time, we did have the first go ahead from God.

His timing on that was perfect too because it was the end of February, and it just so happened there was a five-day workshop scheduled in Whittier, California, in March. An eight-week internship was scheduled in Georgia in April. Bill and I flew back to California in awe and amazement. Just ten days before, we felt like we were going to move to Atlanta and work for Lockheed. Now we were coming back with the strong possibility of going into full-time ministry with Grace Fellowship. This was a tremendous time in our lives of testing and trusting. But again, that's the way our lives had always been, and this was just another step and chapter in our lives and my book. We came back and we both attended the five-day workshop in Whittier. Bill decided to go to the internship which began in April.

Interesting—soon as he made that decision, our house sold. Most houses were not selling, but ours did. Praise the Lord!

The internship was a very intense time. While completing his internship, Bill was staying at the home of our friends where he could totally concentrate and study with no distractions. By the end of the fourth weekend, he came home for a long weekend and some serious decisions needed to be made. Plans were in the process with our house in escrow. The closing date was June 15. It was just in time as the profits from the sale of the business were just enough to last us until June 15. We even sold one of our cars to supplement our expenses and for requirements of training and schooling for the ministry. Yes, we were "laying aside the weights that were holding us back" as it says in Hebrews 12:1–2, and looking to Jesus, our Provider.

During the last month of the internship, Bill and our friend Rita started to seriously look at homes and property for sale. We were amazed at the difference in the cost of living in Georgia. Homes were one-third of the prices of homes in California, and you got so much more for the money. This was very encouraging as our income was going to be in the ministry range, rather than in the business range. We could buy a very comfortable, modest home with insurance and monthly payments much lower than we had in California, and that was what got Bill's attention.

At this point, may I say two things: God really has a sense of humor, and every seven years, I must need another lesson in submission. Picture this (again): we were living in a lovely home in California. A tri-level with five bedrooms, an office, living room, family room, kitchen, dining area, three full bathrooms, a three-car garage, a lovely patio, and a beautifully landscaped yard. Remember too that we were very settled in our church, The Church at Rocky Peak in Chatsworth, and were completely involved in ministry. We were happy, content, and loving every minute.

I had just finished decorating this home. When we moved in, we got a carpet allowance, so we installed peach plush carpet. I had my Winona Lake furniture recovered in white with peach and blue flowered design. I had all of my lamps and accessories repainted peach and blue, which I thought was very creative and conservative. Perfectly placed over the white marble fireplace, I had a large, hand-painted picture to match the flowered design in the sofa fabric. I had just purchased all of my smaller wall hangings and flower arrangements at the California swap meets. Yes, it did look lovely, and I was so proud because I had done it so conservatively this time.

Bill was in Atlanta. Yes, history repeats itself, because one day, I got *that* phone call again—honest! I heard the voice on the other end saying, "Jean, Jean, I found our house." *Oh no*, I thought. *Not again! Could this be possible? Was I hearing things or having a déjà vu experience?*

No, actually, I heard another still, small voice saying, "Trust Me and be still, and know that I am God." *Okay, Lord. I hear you.*

I have to say I have come a long way through the years in this area of submission, especially when I know God is leading. Yes, I'm here to say from *much* experience, it *does* become easier!

So with great excitement this time, I said to Bill on the phone, "You did? Well, tell me what it's like." Again, he began to describe a contemporary, wood-stone-and-cedar house. *What is with these men?* I thought. *Is that all they like—massive, masculine, beamed-ceiling homes?*

"Oh, you'll *love* this one, Jeannie. It's *perfect* for us."

"Okay, I said. "Tell me why," and he began to give me a list of very *logical* reasons why. Not emotional or "feeling stuff," but definitely logical.

It was what we could afford. "Yes, I would say that is the number one consideration," I agreed.

It has just been painted and had a new roof put on. "Yes, that's good too."

It had two extra bedrooms and a loft so we could have room for company and still have an office. "Yes, very good. Tell me more."

It had a complete apartment on the first floor with a separate entrance for Bill's mom, who lived with us. Yes, this was a good feature and extra pluses.

It had a nice lot with lots of trees so it would be shady, and we didn't have too much grass to cut. That was great!

There was no water in sight except for a neighbor's pool. Good. This sounded good.

Bill told me that it was only three miles from the office, and with us having only one car, this would be so convenient. And speaking of convenience, it was very close to shopping areas and grocery stores. Plus, it had easy access to the freeways.

Well, I thought. *What more could I ask for?* Not much. I did ask if I could come down, see it, get a feel for it, and start to think about our furniture fitting and all. So I arrived in Atlanta at the end of May, during the last week of the internship. It was a good time for us to pray and seek the Lord's plan for us, and of course, see "our house." At least, I was a little more prepared this time. Bill had sent some pictures to me. He did a good job of describing and drawing out the plans except for one little thing. He neglected to tell me how the loft "connected" to the rest of the house.

As we drove up to our house, the first thing I noticed was that the driveway was a modified ski slope. Seriously, it angles almost straight up and is about two hundred feet long. *Hmm*, I thought. *This would be fun if we got any snow,* which I thought we didn't. (I want you to know, we did survive the Atlanta Blizzard of '93. In fact, the world looked lovely from our high, mountaintop chalet. We were snowed in for four days.) Anyway, getting back to our first visit to our house, the color was *great*. Not green, but a beautiful beige and lovely complimentary stone on the front. Yes, it had great "curb appeal" as they say in real estate. Of course, you couldn't see too much of it from the curb, as it was so far up the driveway and the tall pine trees covered most of it. I didn't need my bucket of paint out when I got to the door, but I was gasping for air as there were *twenty-eight* stairs up to the front door. *Twenty-eight!* Can you believe it? I said, "There must be an easier way to get up here," and Bill said there was, through the garage.

LET'S SYNCHRONIZE OUR WATCHES, LORD

Whew! I thought. *In a month, we'd either be in great shape, or dead!* (I liked the first choice best.)

We were now standing at the front door waiting for the opening, or the door to open. Bill was all smiles and I was too, by that time. I was wide-eyed in anticipation to see the first glimpse of the inside of our house. As the door swung open, my eyes looked up to the high-beamed cathedral ceiling and this dark, wooden catwalk that went directly across the room, attaching the loft to the rest of the house. *Oh my*, I thought. *This is a little overwhelming when you first walk in, and Bill did neglect to put that in the plans.* He said that he didn't know how to draw it, and I can see why.

However, I got my imaginary bucket of paint out and in my mind, began painting all of that dark wood off-white, like the walls, which were freshly done, I might add. Okay, I got through that scene and very quietly walked through the rest of the house, visualizing where my furniture would fit. Very *quickly*, I said, "Okay, Lord, Here we go again." You see, I've learned over the years when it's time for a lesson. I've learned not to question God's wisdom for long. I knew this was my seventh year—stitch or stretch or switch. Whatever—I was ready for it and very quickly could see a big furniture sale when I got home.

I looked beyond the dark wood and the bare off-white walls, and saw not a house but a home—a home that was perfect for us at this time in our lives. It's a kickback, comfortable, casual, contemporary home that would be open to anyone and everyone who wants to come for care, comfort, and counseling, or just a time to get away and be still before the Lord or all of the above and have fun too. We wanted this home to be a haven for the hurting and a fun place for our family and friends.

With that in mind, I began to decorate and accessorize the house with our familiar things. I took window and wall measurements, and mentally placed what furniture would fit in the proper places. I had in mind to mix my antiques with the modern, contemporary look to soften it up and make it cozy and comfortable—more of a country-contemporary look.

After spending about two hours there, I was ready to go back to California and, once again sell most of my furniture. I put ads in the paper and let everyone at church know: friends, family, and neighbors. We did sell our family room furniture to the people who bought the house, but the rest of my lovely formal stuff didn't sell. The time was getting short, so I put the request on the prayer chain. This was somewhat of a crisis.

As that was being prayed for, we had another unexpected answer to prayer. We had to move out of our house by June 20, and we were not leaving until the first of August. So we were going to rent for six weeks. Oh, just the thought of packing everything up and then unpacking and moving into a rental for six weeks, and then packing up again to make the final move to Atlanta about wiped me out.

But the Lord provided. It was about four o'clock in the afternoon and I was at work, just about to make the final arrangements to rent a house for six weeks, which was going to cost us $2,000.00.

The phone rang, and it was Betty Bross, a dear friend of ours. She said, "What's up? What are you and Bill doing these days?"

I proceeded to tell her and she said, "You can't rent that house for that amount! It's too expensive."

"I know," I said. "But it is the best we can do under the circumstances. Do you have any better ideas?"

"As a matter of fact, I do." She proceeded to tell me that her daughter Sandra and her husband and family were going to Ecuador for six weeks and needed someone to housesit their house—which was on a golf course, I might add. She said, "You could pack all your things and put them in storage because this house has everything. Even linens, dishes, pots, and pans—everything ready to go. You could move in immediately. No down payment, no rent. Just pay the utilities."

I could not believe what I was hearing. Praise the Lord! My heart was pounding, and the tears were rolling down my cheeks. What a godsend! What a friend Betty was! What a plan and what perfect timing!

Again and again, It's God! Glory to His name! With the help of our Prime Time singles group and family, we packed everything up and put it in storage, including my lovely living and dining room sets with all of my beautiful accessories. I could not believe that it had not sold, and I was going to have to take it to Georgia with me. But it was God's furniture, and I rested in that. I kept praying, but rested. We moved into this beautiful, luxurious home on the golf course. It was a decorator's dream—so perfect for our needs, and beyond our hopes and dreams. God does do exceedingly and abundantly above what we ask or think, and He did!

The conclusion of this story reminds me of the Lord selling our house on the twenty-seventh of December—on the very last day! Well, on the very last day when we were loading the truck to make our final move to Georgia, it was about eleven o'clock and the packers were going to be done about one o'clock. I got a phone call from a friend from our church.

"Do you still have that furniture for sale?" he asked.

I said, "Well, it's about to be loaded on the moving truck. Why?"

He said that a young lady in his office was interested in it. I hesitated for a moment and thought, *This is just too funny for words. Is this really happening?* I looked at the phone and heard him say, "Jean, do you want to sell it or not?" I told him yes, I did, but the best I could do would be to bring him pictures because everything was covered and packed. He said okay and told me to come down to his office and that they would be there until noon. I had never been there before, but I found it and got there at noon.

By twelve fifteen, we had negotiated and agreed on a price, and my furniture was sold at the eleventh hour. Really, I drove to the storage place and had the guys deliver the furniture to her apartment. She was happy; we were happy, and again, we praised the Lord for His provisions. Little did we know then, but this was the exact amount we needed to keep us financially afloat from the time we moved until Bill started work in September. God, You are great—and never too soon or too late!

As always, leaving your family and friends is very hard. We were leaving our daughter, son-in-law, and three grandchildren this time and that was very difficult. Not to mention our church family and all of our friends there. We had established some deep and treasured friendships during our seven years there. I think of friends like Dan and Diane Peterson who took us to Cambria when we needed a weekend away before we left. God provided a peaceful place to rest. Through friends of theirs, we were able to housesit for them and enjoyed the quaint, quiet town as we refreshed our minds and spirits, and prepared for our move.

For all of our Sunday school classes and our Bible study who prayed for us, we do thank you. Again, you know who you dear ones are. And we think of the Quigleys who we call our forever friends, and so many more who touched our hearts in a special way.

We had become so close with those we ministered to in our classes and small Bible study group. Yes, this was going to be a very emotional time for us. As I think back, each place and state God moved us through the years has been very special in its own way, and for a different purpose in our lives. Each time and place has been a blessing for us and all of the memories we hold dear to our hearts as we look back and see God's plan being completed in our lives. We were totally overwhelmed as we anticipated embarking on this next journey with Jesus.

I can remember so well the verse the Lord gave us as we left. Jeremiah 29:11 reads, "'These plans I have for you are for good,' says the Lord. 'Plans to give you a future and a hope.'" We claimed that and hung on to each word. In fact, Bill has the piece of paper a dear friend wrote it on and taped it in his Bible.

With that promise, tears in our eyes, and joy in our hearts, we left for our new Atlanta adventure. We experienced exchanged lives across the miles—not only in our hearts and spirits, ministry and new vocation, but in all of the practical ways too. We exchanged:

- Hollywood glitz for the Georgia grits!
- The California rat race for the Georgia slow pace.
- Beautiful palm trees for tall pine trees.
- Heavenly West Coast weather for the Southern humidity.
- Earthquakes for tornadoes.
- Talking fast to the Southern drawl (actually, this hasn't affected me yet. I still have a hard time saying "y'all" slow!)

We had a few adjustments to make and little did we know what we were about to face that first month. As many people who go into full time ministry know, there is always a time of testing. It was no different for us. "Welcome to the ministry," they say. When we arrived, the temperature and humidity was 98 and 100 for days. We were trying to adjust our body temperatures to the extreme change and the constant air conditioning. Bill had a hard time, and by the middle of August, he had bronchial pneumonia and was down for ten days.

He had just gotten over that, and I ended up in the hospital for eight days. In my next chapter, I will share with you how we know that God *allowed* even that for a *purpose* to complete a work in us. He was preparing us for a greater ministry than ever before, but more importantly, a more intimate walk with Him.

Devotional writer, Oswald Chambers, has written:

> Jesus calls service what we are to Him, not what we do for Him. Discipleship is based on ultimate *devotion* to Jesus Christ. A man touched by the Spirit of God suddenly says, "Now I see Who Jesus is," and that is the source of devotion. Today we sometimes are more devoted to causes rather than to Christ. People do not want to be devoted to Jesus, but only to the cause He started. If we are devoted to the cause of humanity only, we will soon be exhausted and come to the place where our love will falter. Our Lord's first obedience was to the will of His Father, not to the needs of men: the saving of men was the natural outcome of His obedience to the Father.

I believe the secret of a contented, committed Christian's life is to know Jesus Christ intimately, be devoted to Him personally, and live for Him exclusively in joyful obedience and service. Christ gave His life for us so He could live His life in us, so that he can live His life through us. We felt like this is what He had called us to do at this time in our lives. We know we are in the center of His will and trust our life's experience will give others *Hope for the Days Ahead*.

Chapter 13

When in the Pits of Pain, Peace Comes Only through Prayer

It was Thursday night, September 3, at about ten thirty, and I was craving something crunchy. It was the fourth day of my diet, and I was doing so well! In fact, I was sure I did not even have anything munchy in the house. But the longer I sat there, the weaker I got until finally, I gave in and went to the kitchen searching for something, *anything* to munch on.

The cupboards were pretty bare purposely, so I wouldn't be tempted, but as luck would have it, way back in the corner of the bottom shelf was an *old opened* bag of tortilla chips one-quarter full. Oh, those looked *so* good to me, but I tasted them, and they were pretty stale. In fact, I could not even chew them because they were so hard. My first instinct was to throw them away. I shouldn't even have been thinking of eating them. But no! That little voice in the back of my head said, "Go ahead. Listen to your stomach. It is making noises. It's hungry."

You're right, I thought, *I am hungry. Let's see. What can I do to soften these chips so that I can eat them?* There weren't very many, and it would satisfy my craving for the crunchies. *Oh, I know! I can put some cheese on them and put them in the microwave. Hmm, that would be good! I'll do it!*

So I did. I sprinkled grated cheddar cheese over the top, covering every single one. I put them in the microwave, and in twenty seconds, I had my feast—scrumptious chips covered with cheese, ready to eat! Hmm, hmm, good!

Well, I kept telling myself they were good. Actually, they were so tough I could hardly chew them. In fact, they went from stale to pulverized, but the cheese was good. And yes, I ate (choked down) every single chip. Oh, my poor stomach! The noises I heard after that were major compared to being hungry. I am sure that empty would have been better than this. It was like eating razor blades with cheese on.

Needless to say, I really had major indigestion. I took three digestive enzymes and about six Rolaids, a Seven-Up, and some Maalox; but nothing helped. I had to sit up and sleep. I could not even lay down. I was so uncomfortable—ouch! What a price to pay for going off my diet!

I will never forget waking up on Friday morning. It was Labor Day weekend, and believe me, I felt like I was in labor all night. In fact, I don't even remember my labor pains being this bad! This was the worst pain I had ever had. It felt like those chips were ripping the insides of my stomach.

Now I have a very high pain tolerance and usually can tough it out. I was trying to do that all day on Friday. I remember saying to Bill, "If I hadn't eaten those stale tortilla chips last night, I would go to the emergency room right now. But I know it was just the chips!" But again, I thought that as soon as I got those things digested and passed through, I would be okay. That tells you what I know about my digestive system. I was pretty miserable Friday night, and the pain did not pass. In fact, it was making me nauseated. I didn't think to take my temperature because honestly, I still thought it was those crazy chips churning around in my intestines—ouch!

During the night, the pain got so bad it literally brought me to my knees praying, "Lord, either take away the pain or take me home!"

I finally woke Bill up to let him know that I was dying! I really thought I was and wanted to let him know where my detailed notes on my "home going" celebration were. He wasn't too excited about finding them at that moment even though they were filed in a colored folder under *Home-going* (quite an accomplishment for a sanguine!). He was more concerned about getting me to the hospital.

I was now on the bathroom floor really getting sick, and I was convinced I was dying. I told Bill, "It's time to call a doctor and take me to the hospital." I told him that if I was going to die. I wanted a Christian doctor attending to me and praying over me.

God really does have our lives planned from the beginning to the end because He knows what we need and when. We had just moved to Georgia, and I wouldn't have known who to call in an emergency. But God knew in April what we were going to need in September. When Bill was in Atlanta completing his internship, Dr. Joe Randell, a Christian Obstetrician-Gynecologist, and his wife, Patti, had loaned him their car for eight weeks, so he was the only doctor we knew. Perfect! Thank you, Lord!

We prayed that Dr. Randell would be home as it was a holiday weekend, and he was! In fact, he was getting ready to speak that morning at a Christian businessman's breakfast right near one of the hospitals where he was on staff. He said he would call and make all of the arrangements and meet us there in about an hour or so. We told him we would pray for him as he spoke, and he prayed for us as we drove to the hospital.

At that point, even though the pain was great, I did begin to have peace. He met us there after he spoke. After many exams, ultrasounds, and x-rays, nothing unusual seemed to show up. My fever and white blood count were up, however, so they decided to admit me. Dr. Joe Randell called another doctor in because they suspected it might be my appendix. All the symptoms didn't fit, so they wanted to watch my blood count and temperature for a while.

I remember meeting Patti Randell, Dr. Randell's wife, for the first time in the emergency room. She came in to encourage me and let me know they would be praying for me. I was so grateful and so humbled. There I was, at my worst, but it did not matter. I had someone praying. What peace! Again, God's provision for a prayer partner and a new friend who is still a dear friend to this day.

They put me in a private room and hooked me up with an IV to give me antibiotics, and that would be my food and drink for a while until they decided if they were going to operate. *Oh well*, I thought. *Back on my diet!* By that evening at six o'clock, my white count had not gone up, and it should have if it were my appendix. The pain was not in the normal place for appendicitis.

The surgeon came in and talked to us. He was very good and very cautious. His advice was to wait and not operate right then. He said that if it was his wife, that's what he would do. I was in good hands, and they were keeping a close watch on me. We were satisfied and knew that yes, I was in good hands—the Lord's.

We called our family and church prayer-chain chairman, my dear friend Tedi Kinney. I know that is what sustained me through the night because I was powerless in pain. I was not prepared for this excruciating pain that truly paralyzed me.

WHEN IN THE PITS OF PAIN, PEACE COMES ONLY THROUGH PRAYER

Oh, how I praise the Lord for my faithful family, friends, and prayer warriors who began interceding for me. Some of you know the great feeling of the power of prayer and the peace it brings. Even though you are still in the pits of pain, you can have that deep, abiding peace and sense of God's presence.

Until that night, I could relate to many other types of pain in life, but not physical pain. I had *prided* myself (watch out for that!) in having a high pain tolerance and that I had hardly ever been sick. In fact, I had been in the hospital only for the births of our three children and one tonsillectomy at age five.

Oh my, I thought. *This is one lesson (a crash course!) I do have to learn and go through so I can empathize and relate to others in pain.* I remember many times in my ministry praying at the bedside of those in the hospital and now I knew, believe me, I knew how they had felt and what they were going through. I would have a whole new dimension of compassion and empathy in this area. It would take on a personal meaning. I remembered the scripture found in 2 Corinthians 1:3–5 where it says what a wonderful God He is. He is the Father of our Lord Jesus Christ—the source of every mercy and the One who so wonderfully comforts and strengthens us in our hardships and trials. And why does He do this? So that when others are troubled, needing our sympathy and encouragement, we can pass on the same help and comfort God has given us. In our trouble, God has comforted us, and this too to help you and to show from our *personal experience* how God will tenderly comfort you when you undergo these same sufferings. He will give you the strength to endure, and He did!

With that comfort, and a sleeping pill, I did get through the night. But as I woke the next morning on Sunday, the pain was still there. They couldn't give me a pain pill because they wanted to know how bad it was. It was bad! When the doctors came in that morning, they ordered a CAT scan to see what was going on. They found that all of my lower organs were inflamed and couldn't even see my appendix. They immediately scheduled surgery within the hour. Dr. Randell was there to assist. He recommended a laparoscopy as it is less difficult surgery, and the recovery is normally quicker.

For my devotions that morning, I had read 1 Peter 1:6, "There is wonderful joy ahead [thank you, Lord, for that promise] even though the going is rough for a while here." (It is rough, Lord. It is!) It goes on to say, "These trials are only to test your faith [Okay, Lord. Consider me tested!] Our faith is far more precious to God than gold… so if your faith remains strong after being tried, it will bring much praise and glory to God."

"Okay, Lord," I said. "My faith is strong, and I trust this will bring You glory."

Again, we called our family, the prayer chain at our church in California, and the staff in Georgia to pray diligently during the next few hours. Dr. Randell prayed for me at my bedside, and Bill and his mom were there also, praying. I went into surgery at peace, claiming God's promises and resting in prayer. In fact, the song in my heart was, "This is my story, this is my song, praising my Savior all the day long." I told the nurses, anesthesiologist, and doctor that they would be covered in prayer. They liked that and so did I.

I expected to wake up from that surgery and have my appendix gone, be pain free, and I planned to go home the next day. *Hmm. Wrong again.* It seems as though God had other plans for me. It's a good thing my life verse is Romans 8:28, "All things are working together for good," because these "things" did not feel good. I was reminded of Proverbs 16:1. It says we can make our plans, but the final outcome *is* in God's hands, although this was not *my* plan.

WHEN IN THE PITS OF PAIN, PEACE COMES ONLY THROUGH PRAYER

The outcome was this: they finally did find my appendix. It was perforated and gangrenous, hidden right behind my ovary. In fact, I was sure they were going to find stale tortilla chips stuck between my large and small intestines! But I was diagnosed as having acute appendicitis. They also determined that my appendix could have been only two hours away from rupturing, which is usually fatal. I am so thankful my life is in the Lord's hands.

Well, for those of you who have had surgery, you know what follows. The pain the day after is sometimes as bad or worse than before. It's just a different kind and in a different place, but nonetheless, it's there! Yes, it was *everywhere*!

Oh my, Monday was miserable. Tuesday was terrible, and Wednesday was worse. I was in the pits again! They were doing everything they could, but at 104 degrees, my fever would not come down. I could not eat. I was dizzy and nauseated, and could not get my strength back even enough to walk.

What could have been a two-day stay ended up to be seven. We called our church prayer chain in California again for more prayer power because I was still powerless. I knew now what it was like to be bathed in and carried through other people's prayers as I was weak and heavy laden as the Bible says. It was a confirmation to me when others have called me to pray just how important it is to be faithful and consistent. "Bear one another's burdens." I knew many, many people were bearing mine, and I know that is what brought me through. I will be eternally grateful.

As always, God did have a plan for my stay. He provided me with an unusual opportunity to befriend and witness to a nurse who took care of me. It was my worst night on Wednesday. I never will forget it. Bill and I just looked at each other in despair. He did not know what to do. I was so miserable, and he had never seen me like this before. We couldn't even talk so we turned on the television. Billy Graham was on, praise the Lord! Some inspiration was just what we needed! The next series of events were very interesting and again, as I look back, they were all planned by God!

We had just called for a nurse because my IV needle had come out of my left hand. In walked a young nurse named Paige. She very confidently began to change it over to my right hand. As she was doing that, she looked up at the television, saw Billy Graham, and said, "My grandmother and mother watch him all the time."

Oh my! A spark ignited in my spirit and I said, "Really? Are your mom and grandmother Christians?"

"Yes," she said. "They pray all the time. In fact, my mom even prays for parking places!"

I chuckled in my heart, and she could see the twinkle in my eyes as I responded, "Really? So do I!"

She said, "You too?"

I knew right then that this was God's plan and appointment for us for that night. I really believe that nothing in the Christian life is an accident or a coincidence. Where we are, what we will be doing, who we will meet—everything is planned by God. This was confirmed in the events that followed.

At that moment, Dr. Billy Graham introduced his special speaker. It was Dr. Damadian who had invented a newer and more reasonable MRI machine. Paige had heard about him and listened intently. I could tell she was interested as he was a professional in her field. His office is near her hometown in Georgia. It was a wonderful story—the testimony of his life and how God uses his professional, God-given talents. I thought, *God, You are so fabulous. You planned for someone to be on the program at just the right time who would be of interest to her, and all of us, really!*

WHEN IN THE PITS OF PAIN, PEACE COMES ONLY THROUGH PRAYER

The events that followed were very amazing. As Paige continued to change my IV to my right hand, she very carefully tried to find the right spot for it so I could be more comfortable.

I said, "Do you mind if I pray that it goes in easy?" (Because my veins didn't always cooperate.)

She said, "No, go ahead."

I did, and at that moment, the needle went right in.

She looked at me and spontaneously said, "I don't believe it!"

I smiled and said, "Believe it! God answered my prayer." I knew she must have thought I was one of those strange Christians who pray about *everything* (and she was right—I do!) And even though this was contrary to her belief, I could tell she believed me, and that was the foundation of our relationship.

As the evening went on, I got worse and that meant I needed more care. So God sent another (angel) nurse to take care of me. Her name was Cheryl, and we became friends too. Cheryl and Paige would alternate taking care of me. I was so thankful for their constant care and concern. Every time Paige would come in, we would talk about our families, life experiences, my faith, and her beliefs. It felt very comfortable to have the freedom to share as we respected each other's feelings.

I have kept in touch with Paige because I know our meeting was pre-arranged by God, and I did feel a special bond with her. When we met weeks later, I asked her why she was so open and listened to what I had to say even though it was not her way or belief.

She said she could be objective because she was not assigned to any religion and was in no way offended or felt manipulated by our conversations. We agreed this was based on our mutual respect for one another. She said that she "observed and saw something in my countenance that was whole and pure." Paige told me that I "was not a religious person, but a spiritual person." She said, "It was like looking in a mirror—the reflection was something inside of you. The way you led your life was an example of something deeper than what you could say." She further told me that the world around me and my circumstances didn't have anything to do with me.

The very day she shared this with me, I found this scripture that confirms what she saw. Second Corinthians 3:18 says, "We Christians have no veils over our faces. We can be mirrors that brightly reflect the glory of the Lord. And as the Spirit of the Lord works within us, we become more and more like Him."

My prayer and desire has always been that people would not see *me*, but would see the Spirit of God in me—Paige's mirror reflection, as it were. I would like them to see Christ in me, lived through me by His power. The Bible says in 2 Corinthians 12:9 that God's power is made perfect in our weakness. During my time of weakness and pain, I am so thankful that His power prevailed and was observed by Paige. She said, "This is what I saw in you, and that made me more open to learn, not about spiritual things (like Christianity), but about my way of life." We never know what an impact or impression our lives may have on others in crises, or our everyday walk of life.

As I look back, I knew two things for sure: that was my worst night of pain and that God used it for His glory as a witness to His power. I know Satan did not like it, and he tried to overpower it, but I claimed, "Greater is He that is in me than is in the world." I have to finish this day's events to give you an idea how the enemy does not like it when we witness and give glory to God.

About eleven o'clock that night, I felt overcome with pain and totally powerless. It felt like an attack from the enemy—like I was losing all of my senses. I felt like I was being consumed by something. I could barely get my thoughts together,

WHEN IN THE PITS OF PAIN, PEACE COMES ONLY THROUGH PRAYER

but somehow, I managed to reach the phone and call one of my prayer warriors in California—Allegra Harrah.

She heard my voice and could tell I was in trouble. When she told me later that it was like Satan was trying to snatch my life away, I shivered because at the time, I didn't know how serious it was. It was serious, and she could sense it. I know she and her husband, Cal, did battle as she prayed for me that night; and with all of my other faithful prayer partners praying, I finally had a breakthrough. The battle was won! I think of the verses in 2 Chronicles 20:15-17 where the Bible says, "Don't be afraid. Don't be paralyzed by this mighty army. For this battle is not yours, it's Gods. Take your place and see the incredible rescue operation God will perform for you. Don't be afraid or discouraged. Go out there tomorrow, for the Lord is with you." Yes, I was rescued. Not by another operation, but by the powerful prayers of His people defeating the enemy. And yes, my tomorrow, which was Thursday, the Lord was with me. I felt a glimmer better and more so throughout the day. By Friday, I felt better yet.

By Friday, it looked as if I was going to be able to go home Saturday. Up until that day, I did not have a roommate, but the hospital had gotten so crowded they were bringing someone in that night. I remember my pastor in California saying, "Jean, it must be someone you will witness to and pray for."

"Yes," I said. "It'll probably be an Italian and believe it or not, she was—and I did! This is not unusual—God has always placed me in the most unbelievable circumstances with Italians, and I love it! I know they are God-planned!

By Saturday morning, I said, "Okay, Lord. I am ready to go home. Please let them discharge me." My fever was down, and I was ready to be released into Bill's care and the comfort of my own home.

Whew! As I look back, it seems unreal, but the reality of it all is very clear. God's purpose is powerful and His plan is perfect. I learned so much in my crash course. I learned about the paralyzing power of pain, but also the profound power of prayer. I learned His plans for us are best. Jeremiah 29:11 states, "These plans I have for you are for good to give you a future and a hope." He always has provisions for us: doctors, hospitals, nurses, people praying. The prayer of a righteous man availeth much. What Satan means for evil, God means for good. Truly, *all* things do work and are working together for good for those who love God and are fitting into His plans.

We know as it says in Jeremiah 11 that our hope is in the Lord, and we *can* have *Hope for the Days Ahead*. His plans for Bill and me at the time of the writing of this book are to be in full-time ministry. We are more convinced than ever that we are right in the center of God's will. We are anticipating the greatest time ever in our lives and service. His plans are best. In Him, we are at rest!

I'm sure many of you are going through or have gone through similar or worse situations and have wondered, "Why, Lord? Why me, Lord? What is the purpose for this pain?" Or maybe you have seen a loved one suffer. He is not a mean and angry God up there saying, "You will suffer today. You will have pain." This is not an accurate picture of our loving, Heavenly Father. But He is sovereign. He knows the beginning from the end. He knows what we can endure and does not give us more than we can handle through Him and His strength in us.

True, He does say, "Pick up your cross and follow Me." But He also says, "My grace is sufficient for you." Sometimes, we will feel like Job, but after all of that, all he went through, he was able to say, "Yea, though they slay me, yet will I trust Him."

Difficult? Yes!

Doubtful? Sometimes!

WHEN IN THE PITS OF PAIN, PEACE COMES ONLY THROUGH PRAYER

Some things we go through here on earth, we will just not understand this side of heaven. But one thing we do know: He loves us with an everlasting love, and He is with us through it all!

There is a song that tells my story and says it all (*used with permission*):

> Through it all, through it all.
> I've learned to trust in Jesus,
> I've learned to trust in God.
> I've learned to depend upon His Word.
> I've had many tears and sorrows,
> Questions about tomorrow.
> Times I didn't know right from wrong.
> But in every situation,
> God gave perfect consolation.
> These trials come to only make us strong.
> So now I thank Him for the mountains,
> I thank Him for the valleys,
> I thank Him for the storms He brought me through.
> For if I never had a problem,
> I wouldn't know He could solve them,
> I wouldn't know what faith in God could do.
> Through it all, I have learned to trust in Jesus.
> I've learned to trust in God.
> I've learned to depend upon His Word!

Chapter 14

Please Send Help, Lord. I'm Really Hurting

I have taken you through the chapters of my life and shared with you the hopelessness, challenges, and crisis in every area of our lives: marriage, family, finances, future, fears, faith, friendships, trusting, timing, parenting, pain, suffering, submission, homes and heartaches, differences, and devastating circumstances. Each one was a very serious and seemingly hopeless situation. Each one was a major crisis and needed to be handled with care. Each one left an indelible impression on my life. Yes, I was hurting. I needed help! Did the Lord send help?

Yes! He sent it through His promises, through His people and through Himself, the Prince of Peace. As I look back, reflect, and reevaluate, I can conclude with this chapter in one of two ways, with a painful "poor me" postscript, or a positive, powerful praise!

By now, knowing my personality, you will not be surprised as to my profound purpose in writing this is to give you *Hope for the Days Ahead*. As I look back at my life, as difficult as it was at times, I can honestly say I know it was God's plan for me. He did have a purpose for it. He made a provision for me. And yes, I can say with great praise that I have peace—the peace that He gives. Not like the world gives, fragile and temporary, but that deep, abiding, consistent peace that takes away our fears and prompts us to put our faith in a living God who loves us. He loves us enough to send His Son Jesus Christ to die for us. Yes, we can have confidence in our crisis when our confidence is in Christ.

Knowing this is the key: no matter what crisis you are in, *Jesus* is the answer. Put your confidence in Him and Him alone. Trust Him. Believe in Him. Receive Him as Savior and Lord of your life. All hope must begin with Him. He is the Alpha and Omega; the beginning and the end; the same yesterday, today, and forever. Jesus said, "I have come to set the captives free." Do you need to be set free from your past, your failures, your sins that wrap around you and hold you back from the freedom that you desire so desperately?

Jesus is the way. John 14:6 says, "I am the Way, the Truth and the Life, no one comes to the father, except through me." He also says, "I have come so that you may have life and have it more abundantly (John 10:10). John 1:12 says, "But to as many as receive Him, to them He gave the right to become His children." The simple truth of the Gospel message is that God loves you and has a plan for your life. Christ died for you and in Him is life itself.

It is not enough to know this. We must repent, confess, and receive Christ in our life. Galatians 2:20 says it all: "I am crucified with Christ that no longer I live, but Christ lives in me. This life I live, I now live by faith in the Son of God who loved me and gave His life for me." Your cure for crisis is to put your *faith* and confidence in Christ.

Here is a simple prayer you can pray:

"Lord Jesus, I love you. I know that I have sinned. I believe You died for me. Forgive me of my sins and for trying to run my own life. I surrender my life to You and receive You as my Savior and Lord. Thank You for the gift of salvation. I place my life, my trust, and confidence in You, right here, right now at the cross. I am laying aside the weights that have been holding me back and looking full into Your face. You, Jesus, the Author and Finisher of our faith, grant me mercy, grace, and peace. I pray this in your name." Amen!

Remember, you did not put your confidence in a *feeling*, but a fact based on the Word of God. When you know the Truth, the Truth will set you free. From this moment, you will be able to expect miracles in your marriage and contentment with your children. Remember, this will not happen overnight, but it will happen as you consistently keep your confidence in Christ and commitment to Him, and seek the advice and counsel of Christian leaders.

As you learn to *trust Him* in your trials and times of testing, *you will grow stronger in your faith*; and soon, your fears will filter through the faithfulness of His promises, especially in the area of your future and finances. *You will have freedom* as you trust Him to supply your *needs* according to His riches in glory. You *will* experience His sufficiency in all things, even in your suffering, His strength *will* be made perfect in your weakness. Yes, *in your pain, you will have His peace* through His power, prayer, and presence. Yes, He *will* heal your hurts and heartaches and turn them into healed helpers, and you *will* experience the joy of helping others. Yes, He *will* send you a friend like Him with arms to hug you. Yes, you will be able to be a faithful friend to someone else. Yes, in this world of hopelessness, you can have victory, freedom, and even fun. Yes, He even brings laughter and humor ("A merry heart does good"). And yes, in even the most difficult circumstances, when we look to Jesus and see our hope is in Him, we can have *Hope for the Days Ahead*.

Meet Our Family

We will celebrate our 60th wedding Anniversary on June 20, 2019. God has blessed us with three wonderful children – Bill – Bonnie – Jay.

Now their families have expanded to three spouses, eleven grand children and six great grand children. We are expecting our 7th great grandchild in July.

MEET OUR FAMILY

Our oldest son Bill and wife Sally have five children and they live in Colorado. Their oldest son Beau and wife Liz have a son Braylon, they are expecting their 2nd child in July. They live in Colorado. Their second son Brett and wife Kristen have two girls, Finley and Avery and have a new brother Miller born in November. They live in Texas. Their oldest daughter Alexandra lives in Georgia and daughters, Ashlyn and Alyson live in Colorado.

Alex, Ashlyn, Bill, Sally, Beau, Liz, Alyson, Kristen, Finley, Brett

Braylon - Finley & Avery
Beau—Liz - Brett - Kristen

Miller
Brett & Kristen

Our daughter Bonnie and husband Dave Blessing have three children and live in Indiana. Their oldest son David has one son, Beauden, David and his wife Lacey live in Indiana. Their second son Jonathan and their daughter Jennifer live in Indiana.

Dave, Bonnie, Lacey, David, Beauden, Jenn, Jonathan

Beauden Blessing

MEET OUR FAMILY

Our youngest son Jay – went home to be with the Lord on July 22, 2016. His wife Denise and their three children live in Michigan. Their oldest daughter Becca is married to Don Markle. They have a miracle baby boy, Noah, who was born @ 22 weeks and weighed 1 lb. 4oz. on January 5, 2018. He is now a healthy 22lbs. Dana their second daughter lives in Michigan and son B.J. is in college in Illinois.

B.J., Jay, Dana, Denise, Don, Becca

Noah Markle

HOPE FOR THE DAYS AHEAD

The Scripture that we have claimed for our family is found in:

Psalm 128 – LB

> "Blessings on all who reverence, trust the Lord and on all who obey Him. Your wife shall be content in her home and look at those children. That is God's reward to those who trust Him. May the Lord continually bless you with all of Heaven's Blessings as well as human joy's. May you live to enjoy your grandchildren."

We do and our great grand children too.

YES – WE ARE BLESSED

TO GOD BE THE GLORY!